Arousing Sense

Arousing Sense

Recipes for Workshopping Sensory Experience

Tomie Hahn

UNIVERSITY OF
ILLINOIS PRESS
Urbana, Chicago, and Springfield

All photographs were taken by the author.

1 2 3 4 5 C P 5 4 3 2 1

♾ This book is printed on acid-free paper.

Library of Congress Cataloging-in-Publication Data
Names: Hahn, Tomie, author.
Title: Arousing sense: recipes for workshopping sensory experience / Tomie Hahn.
Description: Urbana: University of Illinois Press, 2021. | Includes bibliographical references and index.
Identifiers: LCCN 2021021128 (print) | LCCN 2021021129 (ebook) | ISBN 9780252044168 (cloth) | ISBN 9780252086205 (paperback) | ISBN 9780252053108 (ebook)
Subjects: LCSH: Senses and sensation. | Creative ability.
Classification: LCC BF233 .H245 2021 (print) | LCC BF233 (ebook) | DDC 152.1—dc23
LC record available at https://lccn.loc.gov/2021021128
LC ebook record available at https://lccn.loc.gov/2021021129

for Curtis

Menu

* Recipe titles followed by an asterisk work well as online prompts.

List of Illustrations

Acknowledgments

We embody
people, places, things
sensibilities
transforming us
over time
we embody what we practice
and how we practice
lingers

Arousing Sense draws from a lifetime of sensing while practicing, observing, learning, teaching, and playing. It has been a joy to write. Filled with humility and gratitude, I thank the many people who inspired and encouraged me to practice. All teachers, family, participants, students, collaborators, friends, please know you are layered into this book.

Director Laurie Matheson, thank you for the animated conversations that sparked the vision for this spirited collection of recipes. The book came to life because a number of people tested and gave feedback on the recipes; some dared to bring me into their classrooms to playfully experiment. I want to specifically thank a number of inspirational figures for their encouragement; some have been collaborators or "instigators": ethnomusicologist Kay Kaufman Shelemay, who always urges me to push my limits; neuroscientist Alicia Walf, who tirelessly co-taught with me for many years; cognitive scientist and Wild Systems enthusiast J. Scott Jordan;

musician-scholars Junko Oba, Tes Slominski, Fred Maus, Yun Emily Wang, and Pauline Oliveros and the Deep Listening community of teachers; and artists Alex Kahn and Sophia Michahelles (Superior Concept Monsters). I also extend deep gratitude to Ven. Abbot Paul Monshin Naamon, Rev. Tamami Shumon Naamon, and sangha members of the Jiunzan Tendaiji.

Noticing how participants expressively responded to sensory prompts has been moving. The experiences bonded everyone in the moment. After many a class I rolled back to my office, put my head on the desk, and wept, not from sadness but from the surge of energy and enthusiasm reflected back to me from such a simple service of offering sense. Over time, the recipes were tweaked, as participants taught me how to deliver sense. I am honored to have the permission to include works by workshop participants/students Abdullah Alshehri, Katie Boyd, Amelia Farquharson, Safa Koreshi, Michael L. Schrider, Edlyn Terrazas, Katherine Tyrol, and Lorelei Wagner. Thank you.

I dedicate *Arousing Sense* to my husband, composer Curtis Bahn, whose passion for cooking deeply inspired this book. When we first met, he exuberantly cooked our meals, saying, "*I want to cook* . . . cooking is like composing!" Decades later, our lives and the meals continue to be thrilling sensory, artistic encounters. Thank you for your spark and patience.

Author's Note

The bulk of *Arousing Sense* was written prior to the pandemic. Now more than ever, isolated from direct contact, we need our senses aroused. I have noted the recipes that work well as online prompts by adding an asterisk after their titles in the table of contents.

When I was editing the final manuscript, I felt the strong pull to expand upon the relationship of the senses to the deep social concerns that arose at the time—identity politics, racial justice, online teaching, communication, and emotions (specifically fear). I decided, however, that these issues deserved more attention.

Since birth, I have had a wealth of opportunities to be around extraordinary artists, thinkers, and leaders. The inspirations for some of the sensory prompts were sparked by a wide variety of experiences, people, and places. I do not want to mislead readers to think they are entirely my own concoctions. The effort of contextualizing them as sensory prompts is my contribution.

Arousing Sense

1

IMPULSES

Try this appetizer:
Smile so deeply and strongly that your eyes close.

Hear and feel anything?

As you release, notice what stirs in your awareness.

I begin with an impulse, to arouse sense. Even small impulses can stir a wave of excitation, signaling vibration and energy. Embodied poetry. Noticing the stimulus, and any changes in your realm of sensational knowledge, is entirely up to you. Over time, with practice, we notice more. I seek to know how we might teach/learn sense.

Arousing Sense is a simple book of experimental "recipes" for engaging sensory experience. It is for everyone. No specialization needed. Attendance to the vast array of sense can flatten disciplinary boundaries. The purpose of the workshop recipes is to stimulate creative activity by engaging with our senses and to heighten sensory awareness in order to deepen our understanding of what it is like to be human, to be you. Because there is an endless sea of sensory information that we are immersed in, noticing what you are aware of (and what is filtered) reveals and situates your reality, your sensibility. The recipes support workshop leaders and solo practitioners with straightforward instructions for sensory exploration. Being aware of what we sense is the first challenge; using that embodied knowledge to express it is the second. I present several large-scale challenges in this book: how can we expand our modes of expression while heightening awareness? Words are powerful. Before words change our lives, can we allow ourselves to reside in the moment of experience and let the encounter drive the change, sensibly?

Let's awaken, by aspiring to explore, flex, and heighten sensory awareness. Sensory modalities express (manifest) energy and existence differently over time. Can we notice the nuances, then express (convey) what we notice? If we consider that we inhabit different sensory worlds—personally and culturally—then building awareness of the sensibilities *someone else* might be experiencing can expand our knowledge of self/other and open communications. Some sensibilities may be intrinsically subtle, or outside of our own experience, so that we are unaware of them. Deepening awareness, sensational knowledge, supports empathy and encourages compassion. The consciousness starts with the smallest of impulses. Shifting one's sensory point of view, being open, shedding assumptions, and inviting empathy and vulnerability into our explorations can enable deep revelations that what we experience may not be the same as what others experience. Beyond that, how we interpret and respond expressively to experiences can help us to expand, imagine, and notice how we orient ourselves in the moment.

Arousing Sense directs attention to embodied knowledge for exploring the realm of creativity and knowledge making. The recipes are practiced-based explorations and discussions meant to arouse the senses and to "make sense" of how sensory experiences help us to orient ourselves in our environments over time. Let us also ponder what sensory information might be absent, overlooked, or overshadowed because other sensory modalities mask its presence or because of our lack of awareness or sensitivity.

Fostering Transformation

At such a crucial time in history—when contemplative studies and arts, practice-based and praxis-based pedagogy, multiracial pedagogy, feminist pedagogy, communication and intergroup dialogue, intercultural practices, politics of race, critical pedagogy, trauma studies, engaged pedagogy, sensory studies, and student-centered learning (to name only a few!)

have been emerging—I hunger for new possibilities to collaboratively address the harsh political climate and social conflicts. (A sampling of influential books includes those by Ahmed [2012]; hooks [1994]; Freire [2007]; Ergas [2017]; Gershon [2011]; Howes [2005]; Pennebaker and Evans [2014]; Rechtschaffen [2014]; Thompson [2017]; Barbezat and Bush [2014]; Smith [2012]; and Stoller [1989, 1997].) Years ago, I yearned to move these revolutionary theories into the classroom. However, while I held many of these radical, groundbreaking *theoretical* foundations in my storehouse, I realized I had little substance—*actual in-class teaching examples*—to arouse sense in the classroom. I needed to create engaging lesson plans to address even the basic groundwork of communication, *of sensibilities*. For example, how do we engineer vibrant presence in class or workshop settings? Safe discussions that shed light on bias? How can students and teachers, together, find a sense of well-being that fosters transformation? How can we note challenges of difference and propose moving through them together in "radical vulnerability" (Nagar 2019)? How do we create safe, accountable spaces that also offer playful qualities that stir up new experiences and ideas to move everyone to *their* own *edge of vulnerability* so growth can flourish? How can we spark inquisitiveness, curiosity, and creativity alongside emotional well-being? Most importantly, how do we bring the experience of the lived body into the classroom, into research, into our creative work and our writing? How can we challenge what ethnography, art, and creativity is? (See Elliot and Culhane 2017.) The recipes in *Arousing Sense* are meant to engage embodied practices to observe how we think *with the body*. Many recipes in the book develop a sense of community by cultivating shared experiences—"shared," yet again, everyone quickly notices how differently we each experience the world. As Ahmed claims that "to account for racism is to offer a different account of the world" (2012, 3), I offer that bias and assumptions of difference often spark from the smallest of impulses and the interpretations of our sensory experiences.

I want to acknowledge that there are ample resources for creative teaching practices for embodied knowledge from yoga, martial arts, *okeikogoto* (Japanese practice arts), contemplative arts, and other practice communities. The sensitivity of bringing some practices into the classroom can be challenging, due to the implied or very real spiritual nature of some. Note that I do not use the term "mindfulness," not because I am opposed to it but because the word is quite loaded. The popularization of meditation and "mindfulness" has shifted the meaning for some communities, sometimes for positive results. But I would like to be clear that when I run classes or workshops, the point of the exercises is to heighten sensory awareness. Personally, I find the observation of sensory information in time to be profoundly contemplative, yet I reserve this as my own experience and do not impose it on others. When conducting workshops in particular communities focused on contemplative practice, of course my vocabulary changes.

Long ago I discovered that I derive great pleasure from creating prompts and offering them as experimental sensory challenges for others or for my own personal workflow. My childhood was an odd combination of strict discipline in traditional arts juxtaposed with fiercely experimental encounters. Imagine living *inside* or *as* a Dada piece, a Fluxus event, a happening, a pop art scene, or a Zen koan. Welcome to my childhood. My parents, both visual artists with a passion for experimenting and teaching, created a wild, if not bizarre, home life that surely fostered my interest in creating prompts. Fold in my complicated biracial existence (Japanese and German American), one that continues to develop and settle. Elsewhere, I have written about being biracial and how my mixed perspective encouraged and afforded but also blinded me to various insights in my creative, ethnographic work (Hahn and Bahn 2002; Hahn 2007), so I will not detail it here. My family lived on a cliff with fifty-two natural stone stairs leading to our tiny house. Looking back, I recognize that the unusually insular, creative environment atop this cliff stimulated a heightened gaze and sensitivity.

Decades later, my fascination with the transmission of embodied cultural knowledge via the senses, mixed with an upbringing in *okeikogoto*, meditation, dance, experimental improvisation, visual arts, and later Deep Listening, contributed to these recipes and how I teach.

The Importance of Time

Awareness of changes in sensory qualities over time magnifies presence. What sensory changes we perceive and notice directly affects us and our environment but also our perspective of the world—witnessing difference; noting hegemonic structures; sensing climate changes (Silvers 2018); recognizing the situatedness of our lives and relations to others and things; and observing nuances of presence. Recognizing changes allows us to be sensitive to others, to pause, and to consider how to respond and interact. I cannot emphasize enough how strongly the impact of heightened awareness can be on self-awareness, communication, and the sense of connectedness to others and our environment.

Attending to sensory experience pulls us into a contemplation of time, the moment, now. We can notice the state of our personal life and our environment, both local and global. If we are actually focused on encounters demanding heightened awareness, the experience requires that we consider the sensory changes unfurling in time.

As an example, try this:

Directly after reading this sentence, hold your palms against your ears, close your eyes and breathe in and out slowly, and note as many sensory details as possible. (Pause here.)

Although brief, such a pause in one's day can summon a deeper understanding of time, sense, and being. But note, your palms-over-ears moment is *your* particular experience. It emanates from a situated moment and space, including the complexity of who you are, where you are right now, your associations with the activity, and most importantly *the particulars and details of the sensory moment*—the shape and feel of your hands, head, and ears; how you cupped your ears; the blood flow in your fingers; your breathing and awareness. These intimate qualities, and especially what you noted about the experience (or if you continued reading, not pausing to enact the mini experiential experiment), reveal much about you and how you are at this moment in time.

The nuance of sensory encounters throughout our day, if we allow ourselves to be present to them, can provide profound transformations. Considering the potentials for growth through sensational knowledge inspired me to create, research, perform, and teach differently. How might we immerse ourselves in sensory experience and allow the encounter to be unique, to wrestle with language, and in doing so find other means for displaying the nature of what we experience? Seeking alternative means for displaying knowledge has always presented creative challenges for me.

As an explorer of sense, I offer these recipes as performative experiments.

2

MAKING SENSE

In the following passage from my fieldnotes I muse about a voyage to Machias Seal Island Wildlife Refuge, approximately twenty miles off the coast of Maine, to stand inside of a 3′ × 7′ wooden box for the privilege of observing puffins in their natural habitat. Strictly, only a certain number of people are allowed to venture onto the refuge each day.

> **Expanded fieldnotes.** Machias Seal Island Wildlife Refuge, Maine, July 16, 2019. The day began around 6 A.M. in Cutler Harbor, boarding a small boat in two trips to take the group of eighteen to a larger boat, then over an hour voyage out to Seal Island. Luckily, the weather brought no surprises. Although it is mid-July, wearing layers of clothes is important because the trip via boat would be chilly and windy. The seascape offered a wealth of dramatic sensory delights and challenges—sea lions, bald eagles, whales, dolphins, with sun, wind, and salty water whipping our faces, and lapping the boat—but here I'll focus on the blind destination. We'd planned for over six months to be squeezed into the blinds for ninety minutes. "Blind"—what a funny word! Yes, inside the box we were detected less by the outside world, but the sights, sounds, smells, orientation, movements, and general feel inside the dim blind aroused keen new experiences as well.
>
> Once we landed on the island the naturalists recommended carrying a thin dowel pointed upward over our heads while traversing designated paths. We

would quickly note how the highest point (hopefully the dowel tip) endured confrontational pecks from various sea birds, who apparently interpreted our presence as hostile. The naturalists pointed out specific locations where our presence would cause disruption to active nesting. During our visit, for example, terns occupied and fiercely protected their nest on the outhouse roof. After our outhouse visits, the naturalists instructed us to dutifully walk only on designated pathways to the blinds with no stopping for photographs or loitering along the route to minimize bird nesting disruptions. Four of us would occupy our small blind. Once we entered, we would have ninety uninterrupted minutes to observe the surroundings. However, to minimize perturbing puffin habitats, an early exit from the blind meant no reentry. I focused and gingerly walked along the path to the blind, resolved not to be distracted by any alluring puffin commotion. Already our visit posed an abundance of sensory drama.

The wooden blind intrigued me. Painted dull grey, the exterior attempts to camouflage the rectangular box and its human inhabitants among the grey boulders. Although merely constructed from basic pressboard and 2″ × 4″ lumber, the bare, natural wood interior felt warm and rustic. A simple sliding shutter allowed inhabitants to peer out from a number of different views, but we were instructed to keep window shutters closed unless in use. The distinct sensory atmosphere inside the blind emanated from a tangible feature, its repeated use. I noticed the wood was smooth yet also worn below each window—remnants of inhabitants leaning for hours on the wood leaving residual body oils and indentations from heavy cameras or binoculars resting on windowsills. The blind itself embodied the layered presence of its many visitors over the years.

In the blind, a variety of sea birds surrounded us. Literally. Atlantic puffins, as well as razorback auks, landed on the blind roof to congregate, webbed feet creating sharp percussive slapping sounds alternating with a muffled shuffling noise, perhaps from waddling feet. Groups of puffins congregated on top of large boulders just outside the blind, while others peeked out from crevices between boulders as if they had their own sheltering blinds. Often nesting takes place below boulders, and I noticed high traffic and well-guarded areas near such mini caves. The sunny day, enhanced by the brilliant reflection of sunlight from the ocean, green plants, white rocks speckled with yellow-orange lichen, and white excrement, presented a vivid backdrop for viewing sea birds. Despite their small stature, puffin characters loom large. They display white feathers on their torso and black wing feathers. Their comically large bill with bright orange stripes, large eyes, and orange feet contribute to the distinct puffin character. Gazing out from the gloomy blind, I kept marveling at the almost unnaturally flashy orange-colored beaks, eyes, and legs. The smell-scape ranged from a subtle, fresh, and salty aroma, to the pungent, acrid smell of thousands of birds.

The soundscape encompassed a diverse auditory terrain—a continuous lapping of waves, splashes of diving puffins and other water-related sounds, beaks clicking together, wings flapping, a wide array of sea bird squawking, and general cacophony. Loud? Yes . . . and constant. Deafening squawks erupted from the flock when an incoming bird flew in from the ocean with a beak loaded with fish. Curiously, the persistent sound of the ocean, so ever-present and noisy while traveling by boat, became filtered once on the island. I imagine that the muting was partially my own sensory filtering, not only due to my excited anticipation to listen to the chaotic bird chatter and wing flapping, but also because I was now habituated to the wall of ocean sounds. Sensory filtering.

Interpreting Sense

I struggled not to anthropomorphize and overlay my interpretations of what I imagined these small birds might be doing, thinking, and even feeling. But I confess, my attempts to avoid interpreting and characterizing their behavior has not been easy—waddling movements appear comical; flying back from the sea, beaks loaded with sand eels for their chicks, seems to indicate a nurturing side; puffins snuggling together appear lovingly affectionate, and their romping between boulders entertaining. As we cannot assume what another human's experiences or thoughts are at any given time, we surely need to resist such interpretations across species, especially without long-term specialized ornithological field research. My mind understands the logic, but resisting interpretation requires effort. The undertaking poses a number of considerations regarding embodied "knowing," as it acknowledges assumptions based on past experiences and sensory filtering. Because I have lived with "Beakie" (*Cacatua goffiniana*) for over thirty years, particular bird interactions are embodied. I perceive the world through this particular body, through my set of sensory experiences and embodied knowledge. Meanwhile, I'm thinking—weren't the island sea birds also interpreting *our* activities? Were they actually assuming we approached the outhouse to pillage nests? A paradox of "nested" philosophical interpretations of interpretations abound. But I digress. Let's return to the blind journey.

Unfortunately, someone on the boat loudly declared that puffins and razorbacks *sound like chainsaws* revving up. The "sounds like" comparison conjured countless personal sonic memories of chainsaws for me. Then, when I heard the actual cacophony of these sea birds, I found it difficult to shake the sonic translation foisted upon me prior to my lived encounter. 'Twas a sensory spoiler alert that would impose upon my first sonic acquaintance with puffins—a mere suggestion of an auditory memory, or schema, that would initially not allow me to experience the actual puffin and razorback chatter. Stolen sensory encounters. However, once in the blind I found the sound world deeply moving and transformative—so unlike one thousand chainsaw artists or horror flick maniacs surrounding our blind. More importantly, the auditory experience constituted only a fraction of the lush sensory immersion, alongside the movement, smell, feel, temperature, light, emotion, and so on. The parsing of the senses, while a convenient means for organizing observation, tends to compartmentalize such a truly elaborate world of sensory experience. Qualia.

I often wish that language did not impose on an initial experience. The human capacity to use language, paired with our tendency to compare new experiences with the past, helps us to communicate and grow. Schemas—frameworks that represent experiences, categories, and patterns that we have previously encountered—help us to discern, learn, and broaden our sensory vocabulary and provide a theory of learning through information processing and comparative judgments. Growth arises through a perturbation of previously experienced schemas. Sure, I understand the concept, yet it provides me with little solace while entertaining chainsaws and puffins.

Arousing Sense, Situating Sense

Immersion in the lush puffin island sense-scape engaged and intrigued me, arousing a blissful wonder. But why am I telling you this story? And why am I disclosing my frustrations and bliss at the opening of *Arousing Sense*?

Sensory experience orients us in the world. The senses situate us directly in a location and in the moment, as sensory experiences occur and change over time. The more sensory impressions that arise and are noticed, the greater the memory imprint of that moment, event, environment. Sensory experience is essentially about communication—transmission between our bodies and the environment, other individuals, and the interior landscape of our bodies. What we sense and what we make of an experience reflexively reveals who we are, our environment, and our culture. I value how attention to qualities of sensory experience conveys both our individuality and our connectedness to our environments and other people and beings, if we are able to note our differences and similarities through our experiential engagements.

How does sensory information provide cues for where we are in time and space? Or when a dish we are cooking is ready? Or burned? Sensory qualities punctuate time and instill memories, such as an alarm ringing, a cricket chirping in the summer, or incense burning during a ritual. These cues orient us deeply; our accumulated experiences define who we are.

While *Arousing Sense* is not heavily theoretical, I'd like to frame how the senses are approached in the text, relative to the body and experience. Reflexivity supports transparency. Identifying who is writing and why, from a clear voice, helps readers frame the text and to attempt to comprehend the perspective from the author's point of view.

First, for transparency, I would like readers to know that (aside from my personal background provided earlier) my academic training is in ethnomusicology, dance/movement scholarship, and music and dance performance. I have been a long-term meditator and for a dozen years have been collaborating internationally with artist-scholars in contemplative arts and sensory studies and with cognitive scientists and neuroscientists, specifically addressing embodied consciousness and non-duality of mind and body. This blended background undoubtably tints the way that I move within theory and practice. Traveling and collaborating between these disciplines has been an intense learning experience, as terms used in different disciplines needed to be "translated." I am optimistic and grateful—fascinated by the body, senses, experience, and embodiment—that everyone comes to the table with nourishing contributions.

If multisensory approaches to research and creative endeavors are acknowledged, disciplinary boundaries blur. I propose that theory needs to follow experience and practice. Rather than clutch a theoretical approach and proceed to apply it to an experiential encounter, theory needs to arise from the wealth of experience, artifacts, creative output, fieldnotes, interviews, conversations, and so on. Each project deserves a theory well-suited for the particular material, the culture, and time period. Applying a theory that provided insights two hundred, even twenty, years past might be interesting, yet how relevant is it today? Likewise, the inappropriateness of applying a Western theoretical model to a non-Western culture's art making, practice, or experience.

Sensory experiences never occur in a vacuum, devoid of social, cultural, and environmental filters, insights, patterns, language, or emotions, simply because the person sensing embodies a cultural and personal background. As an ethnographer and artist, I support a *culturally situated* and *culturally theorized* understanding of what "experience" is. In other words, how is the sensory encounter conceptualized within the given cultural context? We need to take into account the individual who is sensing the experience or building the sensory experience for others. For ethnographic projects as well as creative projects, what are the indigenous theories that serve the community, the culture? It has troubled me that a great deal of past scholarly research has ignorantly overlaid outside approaches and theoretical perspectives onto another culture's practices, without comprehending the depth of knowledge, insights, or even acknowledgment of the particular culture area's theoretical concepts, views, or approaches.

To be insensible—unconscious and unaware—of other peoples' sensibilities dismisses the rich diversity of our world, our humanity. What an egregious failure such an insensibility embodies, holding a presumptuousness that supports colonialist, orientalist, or single culture–dominant theoretical mindsets. All cultures have indigenous theories, perspectives, and practices regarding the senses, experience, and the body. The theory may not be in the scholarly form that academics are accustomed to, but it is our responsibility to ask, to notice and practice, in order to comprehend.

I invite readers to consider the myriad cultural contexts that they (and the participants in their workshops) embody and how each individual's notion of experience contributes to their unique understanding and framing of their own world (Smith 2012). For this reason, I do not propose or advocate for one specific theoretical model in this book. Depending on the background of the reader, particular words may unintentionally trip theoretical wires. I ask readers to suspend their framing of terms and be as open(-minded) as possible when offering or attending workshops. Of course, I carry my own baggage reflecting my era and upbringing. I hope my reflexively transparent, very personal disclosures help to frame my humble suitcases.

Making-Contemplating

There's something about the making-contemplating cycle that fascinates me. There's something about the iterative, cross-pollinating flow between creativity and research that offers a precarious edge to explore how art making and research inform each other. There's something arousing about sensing the world and attempting to creatively make sense of the experience. Making and thinking need not be separate endeavors. Often separated into creativity and research, let us notice that there is creativity in research and research in creativity (Barrett and Bolt 2007). Making and contemplating are engagements of embodied consciousness in practice. In the past, ethnographic research has tended to be a top-down undertaking, in contrast to most creative endeavors that are built from the bottom up. "Top-down" here means engaging in research of an existing culture, in contrast to creative endeavors that begin from scratch ("bottom up"). *Arousing Sense* proposes that creativity has the potential to exist in all endeavors, depending on the dynamics that are in the mix. In summoning creativity in research, one needs to peer deeply into the ethical dynamics of the particular research, to scrutinize one's reasons for displaying knowledge in particular forms, and reflexively understand one's relationship to the culture, land, individuals, community, and work.

Lived experience and practice can be a means for comprehending how embodied practices contribute to consciousness, specifically contemplative and embodied consciousness. I want to know how we can sense and observe sensory-rich experiences and incorporate them into our research, creative process, and understanding of culture. Practices that involve the body have the potential to reach into our deepest core, whether we consider our sensory endeavors for art making, research, contemplation, philosophical or personal introspections, or other purposes. I want to know how culture becomes embodied knowledge. Over the years—while researching Japanese traditional dance, Monster Truck rallies, Deep Listening, gestural controllers for performance, sense-scapes, or improvisation—particular sensibilities were revealed *as the vehicles* for embodied knowledge. I am fascinated by the senses, transmission, and how we teach and learn through the body and how the body continues to teach us.

Teaching Sense

How do we teach and learn from sense? More specifically, how might we lead a group through sensory realms, to examine and question experience, and arrive at sensational knowledge—the wisdom of the body? Can we reach beyond dualities? Can we reach beyond (false) constructs of only five senses to include other sensory modalities? How can we reveal culturally constructed sensibilities? How might we convey the potential profundity of sense without stating the obvious, "This is going to be a deep experience"? Much like "puffins sound like chainsaws," a trite communication abducts the lived impression, the attention to the situatedness, the pleasure of sensing, and the wealth of immersive sensory experience. However, come to think of it, the "puffins sound like chainsaws" analogy proposed a surreal pairing of two sensory worlds that I might not have juxtaposed and tackled. My struggle set out new realizations, new sensational knowledge.

Serving Sense

I offer you a simple book of recipes for workshopping sensory experience. Here I arrive at the core of *Arousing Sense*. Offer experience. Offer sensory encounters. Offer experiences in a wide variety of recipes that flexibly suit a leader's background and the particular context—sometimes offered with playfulness or with performative drama, seriousness, or mystery. Serve sense, step back, and observe how differently or similarly participants experience the encounter. Repeat. Sound simple? Yes, and profoundly moving. *Arousing Sense* is a collection of experimental recipes for engaging sensory experiences. The recipes support the contemplation and cultivation of creativity and ideas through prompts and challenges. While the recipes tend to be playful, do not be deceived. In fact, dare to go deeper. It is the very nature of playfulness that allows for a loosening of self to increase insight, empathy, and vulnerability.

Why use "recipe" as a model? Cookbook recipes tend to fall into concise, step-by-step formats that are easy to follow while cooking. The purpose of this book is to support leaders with instructions for sensory exploration that are straightforward and effortless. Because the hard work lies in your workshopping sensory encounters, I realized that only the basic inspirations, tips, and sequencing would be necessary. It is your task to select your ingredients, chop, taste, simmer, taste, smell, blend, taste, plate, and dine. Like cooking, the entire process of concocting and serving a workshop specifically for your group can be a pleasurable, nourishing experience.

Outside of the pragmatic advantages of a recipe format, I have been inspired by the profound qualities of embodied sensibilities in the process of cooking as a model. Recipes convey sequence and timing. Preparation of a meal can be a full-body sensation of smells, temperature, textures, movements, tastes, touch, a balance of spices, observing liquid and solid qualities, and so on. Sensory chemistry. Even better, sensory experiences unfold and change over time in our everyday lives—while cooking, eating a meal, or making art. There are rhythms of sense in our lives that fuel our bodies and memories.

I envisioned the recipes for a wide variety of purposes—as prompts for generating ideas for practice-based research and creative endeavors, to develop a personal practice, and for conducting sensory studies or fieldwork "warm-ups." Regarding sensory studies "warm-ups," I propose that practicing an awareness of diverse sensory realms can heighten one's sensory attendance prior to doing fieldwork. In addition, I offer these recipes as performative adventures. Please be wild exploratory chefs, nourish yourselves, and feel free to transform the recipes in ways that suit your purposes and particular settings. I conceptualized them as living recipes that can develop over time as needs change.

Vulnerability

Always hold vulnerability as a key to unlock sensational knowledge. Be existentially open. Resist defining. How else might we step outside of ourselves and allow for experience to be fresh? How else can we remind ourselves that it is human to want to compare, to name, to use language, yet also grapple with the directness of sensation? How else can we tame one's control mechanisms in teaching and respect the experiences of others? Allowing ourselves to be vulnerable, we have the potential for sensory experience to profoundly change and transform us.

The participants in your group will feel vulnerable to different degrees. The challenge is to find ways to offer a supportive space so that they feel comfortable with various levels of vulnerability—or, feel comfortable with discomfort! Vulnerability can be terrifying, yet it offers potentially liberating insights. When we step into the liminal space of the unknown, a sense of vulnerability might make us quake. The momentary sensibility of feeling unsure can unveil our thresholds so we can acknowledge them, test boundaries, and lead us to experience the thrill of experimentation.

When researching and writing *Sensational Knowledge* (2007), I faced vulnerability full on:

> If we are able to reveal and monitor our vulnerabilities, the dynamics of power and control issues that play out in ethnographic practice can be incorporated as part of the work. In her book of essays, *The Vulnerable Observer: Anthropology That Breaks Your Heart*, Ruth Behar reveals the diversity of vulnerabilities encountered by anthropologists and writes:
>
> > Anthropology . . . is the most fascinating, bizarre, disturbing, and necessary form of witnessing left to us at the end of the twentieth century. As a mode of knowing that depends on the particular relationship formed by a particular anthropologist with a particular set of people in a particular time and place, anthropology has always been vexed about the question of vulnerability. (Behar 1996, 5)
>
> In the ten pages following this quote Behar provides examples of vulnerable moments exposed by reflexivity, and then cautions, "Vulnerability doesn't mean that anything personal goes. The exposure of the self who is also a spectator has to take us somewhere we couldn't otherwise get to. It has to be essential to the argument, not a decorative flourish, not exposure for its own sake" (15). (Hahn 2007, 10; for more on reflexivity, see Hahn 2006)

Insights can arise through sensory examination; we merely need *to really be there*—aware, vulnerable, resilient, and cultivating curiosity in the moment. I invite you to try my recipes and, while incorporating your own spices, locate your own vulnerabilities, notice edges of your safe zones, and observe that participants have their own edges as well. Asking participants to notice their ever-changing edges of vulnerability is vital. Offering a cultivation of awareness—of sensibilities, tendencies, vulnerabilities—moves those edges out farther to enable a freeing, liberating sensibility.

Be transparent about process. Encourage transparency. No skimping on spices. Leaving ample time for collaboration and discussion in each session fosters self-discovery of the idea that sensory experiences vary between participants. I notice how sharing experiences through discussion and collaborations cultivates bonding, empathy, and a positive, supportive learning environment. One of the most important challenges for leading a group, however, is to find a way to establish a safe yet challenging environment to enable creative experimentation.

To grow and seek new ways of expressing oneself, establishing a sense of safety for fostering vulnerability may be necessary. For example, in most classes, there tends to be a continuum of extroverts and introverts. My challenge is to find ways to shepherd the group into a balanced state, where the extroverts, introverts, and everyone in between can thrive and be curious together. A humble approach of strength through humility, play, and experimentation seems to work in many of my contexts. These approaches apply not only to the participants. I strongly encourage "leaders" to model a humble and playful stance while leading their group. I know, you are probably asking, "How can a *leader* lead vulnerably and with humility?" Seem counterintuitive? While "leading" a group with such a stance may feel awkward in the beginning, I urge folks to take small steps to the edge of experimentation and vulnerability. Better yet, allow yourself to fall down. Willingly leading a group by personally walking the edge of failure during experimentation can model the kind of creative experimentation you hope for a group. Safe, accountable spaces often present themselves through a leader's humility and observance of wonder. Curiously, the edges that determine safe and accountable spaces expand as we grow, and new edges of confidence can develop. Here is where the humanity of being alive—sensing, collaborating, noticing egos, noticing control, facing the frailty of existence, being human—can liberate and encourage others in a group to dive in and find their own edge. That is leading. And where does it begin? Your own personal practice.

Personal Practice

I propose that active, focused engagement with activities that heighten sensory awareness of one's self, of one's environment, of one's entire body, and of the relationship between body and environment can stimulate the creation of new knowledge. For most of the recipes and exploratory challenges I serve, I ask everyone to let go of expectations, intentions, and goals. Allow me to explain . . .

I often teach courses related to creativity. As an ethnographer, I study the ways people are creative, so I am aware that creativity flourishes only from regular practice. Creativity is tricky; I find it is something one can encourage, model, inspire, or trick someone into doing. Years ago, I made a pact with myself to set up a daily practice. It doesn't need to be an enormous endeavor, but it needs to happen *every day*, just like eating, just like meditation. If I'm about to go to bed and realize I haven't done anything creative all day (which of course is relative), I grab one of the sketchbooks that sit by my bedside and write a few words that will become a poem tomorrow, or swipe a few meaningful strokes on paper, or get up and take a few photographs, and so on. I dare you to try this for even a week. Really. I guarantee that the challenge will affect you.

The only way I can continue my promise to myself is to remain humble in my lack of intention and expectation. You read correctly: *lack* of intention and expectation—*no* specific goals exist, except to generate a creative space, and I have *no expectations* for brilliance. I imagine, if only one out of one thousand creative moments reveal even a small insight, then I am fortunate. The practice is generative. Later, there is time to build upon these sparks, to plan and develop large projects. But my daily intention remains to foster awareness, creative practice, and sensational knowledge.

My activity needs to lie outside of my normal creative routine for me to be disoriented in a sensory way. In my book *Sensational Knowledge,* I explored notions of orientation through disorientation for embodied practices: "Orientation through dis-orientation occurs as a disruption of normalcy, followed by a clarity that signals a re-orientation and comprehension of one's sense of place, literal or otherwise" (2007, 154). In my daily creative space I attempt to try something new, playful even, that disrupts my sensibility of being oriented and stable. I seek pathways that mess with my sensory order. By trying something different, there is potential for returning to my daily life with a different perspective, or with new potentials for knowledge building. The senses and body are stretched, and there is growth.

Returning to the idea of leading a group through a creative exploration, I hope my invitation reveals how your own outward display of experimentation and exploration—*if only through an embodied stance*—can model and provide a safe space for vulnerability and greater experimentation. It begins with the leader, the guide. If you actively practice creative explorations in your everyday life, believe me, the groups you guide will certainly know through your energetic presence. They will understand that you are working on your own practice, your vulnerable, human edge, and the practice will energize them to do so as well. Everyone needs to try falling down now and then to discover boundaries and resilience while playing with gravity. Why not lead while also creating a connection with the groups you lead?

How to Use This Book and Recipes

This section describes the layout of the book and recipe format. "Impulses" and "Making Sense" introduce readers to the interdisciplinary, multisensory aims of the book. Because disciplines should not be divided by modalities of sense, interdisciplinarity is key. Being expressive in increasingly diverse ways is liberating and expands our humanity. The core of *Arousing Sense* is the thirty-four recipes in the "Tantalizing Recipes" section. They range from engagements of sound, movement, touch, and smell to shifting perspective, memory, time, absence, pareidolia, and so on. "On the Go" is a collection of six quick and easy recipes for workshops. "Dessert" includes two short examples of my own experimental "recipe" texts. The "Resources" section provides a brief explanation of freewriting as a writing practice, followed by inspiring writing examples by workshop participants in response to specific sensory prompts. The last section, "Cordial Closure" (a nod to after-dinner cordials), provides some parting thoughts to the menu.

I attempted to keep a similar form for recipes, for convenience. The sections of most recipes include a backstory and overview; notes on preparation required; recipe steps; notes to the leader; post-exercise discussion topics; and applications for sensory studies (fieldwork) and creativity. For easy reference, the section "How to Use This Book—a Quick Review" presents an overview of the recipe format.

Note that each recipe title in the Menu (the table of contents) is followed by a few words describing the general focus of the workshop exploration. Hopefully, these few words serve as a basic key to help those in a pinch for a lesson plan or for locating nourishing personal practice efforts. The "Overview" sections within the recipes expand upon these brief descriptions so that leaders can determine the appropriateness of a recipe for their purposes.

"Backstory" sections reveal how I concocted a recipe. Feel free to read these odd personal stories to the class. However, I suggest they be read after your workshop session, since I often divulge why I was moved to compose the lesson plan or potential outcomes. Knowing what a leader hopes or aims for an exercise ahead of time often skews a group's focus and does not encourage participants' own inner struggles to find personal meaning in the sensory prompt. If appropriate, you may want to relate your own parallel story to bring participants closer to you and add excitement to the exploration.

Warning: I endeavor to be as opaque and obtuse as possible, specifically to prompt interpretation. I realize my predilection for practices sparked by ambiguity and absurdity can be frustrating for participants (particularly those who desperately need to know exact outcomes and grades), but I am stubborn about the need for inner struggles to forge expressivity, musings, and new ideas (Zeki 2006). The outcome is never as important as the process and practice of arriving.

Next is the "Preparation" section, letting leaders know what ingredients are necessary, including what needs to be prepared or purchased prior to the workshop. Have you ever arrived at a class and realized that your class plan for the day needs to be postponed? Or perhaps you were unable to prepare anything for class? It happens to everyone. If you find yourself in such a tight spot, use the recipes in this book that require no or minimal preparation. In desperate times, check out the "On the Go" chapter for quick recipes you can use after only a quick glance.

Recipes often include an "Opening Announcement," written in such a way that you can simply read it to the participants directly from my text. Be performative. Some leaders find comfort or enjoyment presenting some of the wackier recipes through my textual voice (taking the pressure of oddity off of the leader). It can offer a kind of double presence, where I am leading the group experiment from afar and the leader becomes part of the group. The specific steps of a recipe come next, including "Note to Leader" sections for teaching tips and suggestions.

The next section, "Post-Exercise Discussion Topics," lists a range of topics that commonly surface in group discussions. I have been pleasantly surprised by some of the themes that have emerged, so I provide them as a way to help you unpackage the exercise and anticipate topics that pop up.

The final two sections of the recipes reference two broad disciplinary settings—"Sensory Studies and Fieldwork" and "Creativity"—to summarize the general benefits of the particular recipe when used in these disciplinary settings, such as flexing one's sensory awareness (prior to doing fieldwork) or generating ideas for creative work. While I target these two disciplines, the recipes in this book can be incorporated into a wide range of workshops, including creative writing and composition, creativity, art making, movement exploration, contemplative practices, communication, improvisation, collaboration, teamwork, and ethnography and fieldwork, to name a few.

If leaders expect a finished product from participants, such as a final paper for a university assignment, then the recipes offered here can be employed as generative prompts that support a first draft. When I taught with neuroscientist Alicia Walf, we offered sensory prompts every week, leading to first drafts (or creative projects) that we commented on, then the final works were due at the close of the semester and were also presented live to the class. In addition, during the semester Professor Walf would provide short general lectures on particular sensory organs (such as the olfactory system).

The recipes in *Arousing Sense* pair well with a wide range of texts, depending on your purposes. A few examples would be Pink's *Doing Sensory Ethnography* (2015), Le Breton's *Sensing the World: An Anthropology of the Senses* (2017), Heywood's *Sensory Arts and Design* (2017), Stoller's *Sensuous Scholarship* (1997), Classen's *Worlds of Sense: Exploring the Senses across Cultures* (1993), Howes and Classen's *Ways of Sensing: Understanding the Senses in Society* (2014), Howes's edited work *Empire of the Senses: The Sensual Culture Reader* (2005), Porcello and his colleagues' article "The Reorganization of the Sensory World" (2010), and Bhattacharya's *Fundamentals of Qualitative Research: A Practical Guide* (2017). *The Fluxus Performance Workbook* (Friedman, Smith, and Sawchyn 2002) would also pair well. Contemplative studies practices vary widely, depending on the practice (meditation, yoga, martial arts, Deep Listening, and so on), so I will only offer that the recipes here can provide a group with a different kind of contemplation, one that might offset or complement one's regular practices.

Underlying Themes in Practice-Based Explorations

The prompts tend to fall into several categories to initiate exploration: quick-recipe prompts; experiential, sensory-rich prompts; and instruction prompts. All are based on the approach of learning through doing. While "cooking," you will notice underlying themes and patterns that arise organically.

A few examples:

- Offer a sensory experience with minimal explanation (only the process), followed by time for mapping out work such as writing, drawing, moving, or some other activity. Finally, encourage group discussion to share observations and creative process.

- Writing with lush, sensory-rich language draws readers' attention. Providing the details of an encounter helps to convey the depth of one's particular experience. See the pieces by Schrider and Farquharson in the "Resources" chapter for examples of sensory-rich writing.
- Participants are noticeably excited and engaged when mystery abounds. Many recipes kindle mystery through enhancing anticipation, curiosity, and surprise. Performatively incorporating these states enhances the "plating" or delivery of sensory recipes. Providing moments of performativity, not only for the leader but for participants to engage in experience as research, experimentation, and performance practice, can be one way to engage mystery.
- The incorporation of uncommon or odd juxtapositions in presentations urges us to creatively make associations and linkages. Unconventional juxtapositions can raise curiosity. "Making sense" of unexpected combinations forces everyone to think outside of our boxes or to break habits. Why is an acorn sitting next to a metal bell? We tend to contemplate why something (or a concept) arises in an unexpected context and to struggle and ponder new connections between things and contexts.
- The regular inclusion of freewriting and discussions helps to generate ideas and material, process experience, find meaning, or tease out how we sensed or created something. (Note: If you are not familiar with freewriting, please see the "Resources" chapter.) For all my diatribes about how language can abduct sensory experience, I feel strongly about the attempt to "make sense" of experience through the art of writing *after* a sensory experience. Freewriting, with no expectation of brilliance, tends to percolate ideas through open-ended considerations. Freewriting may not produce a complete text, but interesting ideas for a piece can emerge. *It is the generative practice that matters.* Freewriting also sets aside space and time in the classroom or workshop for contemplation and wonder.
- Similar to freewriting, I often request "freedrawing," including doodling and sketching. For some participants, assigning words to experience can be daunting. Periodically ask everyone to draw instead of freewrite, *or* mention that freewriting, freedrawing, or both are encouraged.
- Discussion after a freewrite or freedraw is vital. Freewriting/freedrawing supports discussion because "something" has been articulated on paper, helping participants to go the extra step to be present with, and verbally share, something from the newly written text. The discussion propels the generative environment forward. At this early stage, participants are most receptive to comments and are less

likely to be defensive, simply because their work is still fresh and unpolished.

- Everyone is creative. I cannot stress this enough. Participants often declare, "I'm not creative!" Without singling out that person, I take the opportunity to talk about vulnerability and growth, or how creativity has a range of meanings (not just in the arts) and everyone, regardless of "artistic" background, has creative capacity. Here's a chance to discuss the notions of innate or natural "talent" and how the senses, body, environment, culture, and especially practice factor into creativity and ability. Readings on creativity, flow, plasticity of the human brain, and human growth in a variety of fields can easily be paired with recipes.
- Collaborations can be great enablers for practicing the basics of communication; shifting points of view; stirring up habits and well-worn paths; extending oneself; building empathy; finding we are not alone; and discovering that we experience or emphasize different sensory worlds. However, collaborating can also be frustrating for those who like to call all the shots and claim authorship. Prior to a collaborative prompt I often point out the benefits of noticing one's tendencies to dominate, follow, hesitate, or be reactive while working together. Collaboration can help everyone get out of their regular mode of behavior and be more generous.
- Collaboration and improvisation tend to expose a range of tendencies specifically related to communication and social skills. For example, you will notice in some (either others or yourself) an inability to be open-minded about where a collaboration leads. The individual may attempt a number of controlling or coercion tactics or embody impatience, make assertions, and even display tantrum-like behavior. Others in the group may cringe or pull back. I usually point out to a group that clearly yet sensitively voicing a suggestion for creative possibilities during collaboration/improvisation is good form, but heavily editing, "correcting," or changing others' contributions can cause turmoil. What a wonderful opportunity to mention how such behavior moves the process away from collaboration. The challenge is, how can we point out in a positive and generous manner that the disruptive behavior or lack of flexibility does not contribute to collaboration? The "doesn't play well with others" caution sign looms large.
- Claiming ownership versus partnership relates to the above example. The two do not always emerge together, however. I find it interesting that collaborative activities can precipitate possessive tendencies, challenging me to find ways of articulating or modeling positive collabora-

tive practices in a session. I believe there are opportunities for pointing out how creative collaborations put a magnifying glass to social practice and agency. Merely noticing one's own impulses, or even biases, *enables freedom*.

- Some recipes lend themselves to developing one's individual practice; others work well in group sessions. I encourage individuals who want to take on explorations originally intended for groups to creatively alter the recipe for their needs. Some recipes emphasize collaboration. If that is not feasible, then devise ways to work solo. The same for recipes written for solo exploration. In some cases, I provide suggestions on how to transform the recipes between solo and collaborative work, or to start with one type of approach and segue to another.

How might we spark insights and creative work from sensory experiences? I long to comprehend deeper qualities of sense and the introspective nature of qualia.

Welcome to my table.

3
HOW TO USE THIS BOOK—A QUICK REVIEW

Most recipes follow a consistent form. This section presents a quick glance of the recipe format.

Name of Recipe

Overview (or *Backstory and Overview*)

This section serves up a narrative of how the recipe came to life, followed by a brief overview of the recipe.

Preparation

Notes any pre-workshop preparation or information needed, including workshop space and materials.

Recipe

OPENING ANNOUNCEMENT

Written in a voice that can be read directly to participants, the opening announcement provides an introduction of the recipe for your group.

STEPS

The step-by-step narrative stages of the recipe.

Note to Leader

If any asides for the workshop leader are necessary, they are listed here.

Post-Exercise Discussion Topics

This section notes a range of topics that often arise in workshop discussions.

Sensory Studies and Fieldwork

Includes comments relevant for using this recipe for fieldwork workshops.

Creativity

Includes comments relevant for using this recipe for creativity workshops or personal practice.

4
TANTALIZING RECIPES

Orienting Ritual

Backstory and Overview

"Orienting Ritual" (originally "First Orientation—The Body in Text") is an excerpt from my book *Sensational Knowledge: Embodying Culture through Japanese Dance* (2007, 19–21, Wesleyan University Press). It does not conform to the outline of the other recipes in *Arousing Sense*, yet because it inspired the book, I offer it here.

Imagine taking a drink of water from a glass *as* performance. I employ this engagement to locate a regularly repeated experience shared by readers to be utilized as a unit of observation. How can we convey the essence of movement, sound, and the lived experience of culture? How do we write the body into text?

Probably you raise the glass and drink "without thought"—without the need to consider or analyze each action methodologically. But if this ritual were a research project, those unconscious aspects held in your embodied knowledge would hopefully surface as your examination progresses and as you find empirical substance in the activity.

First, let's consider the unit of observation, or define the edges of this ritual. In your eyes, when does the "performance" start and end? Does it begin when you enter the kitchen (if this is indeed where you perform "the act")? How often do you repeat this ritual? Is there a pragmatic aspect to this performance? When did you learn this behavior and from whom? What are other considerations? Finally, and my point behind this exercise, *how can you convey the enactment* of the ritual to an outsider of this tradition so that she can deeply comprehend it? If the outsider were standing next to you, wouldn't it be easier to take her to your special ritual area and show her? How about conveying the experience in text? Not as easy as demonstrating, right?

Imagine your water ritual as a deeply moving artistic "tradition" that you need to transmit through writing. How would you convey not only the rudimentary steps of the ritual but the context and embodied experience of the art? Consider the negotiations of turning on the faucet and filling the glass with water—how do you coordinate the movements? Can you describe *in detail* your grasp and coordination of the glass as you bring it to your mouth? Then, do your lips move in preparation as the glass approaches? Do your glands react in expectation? How do you draw the water into your mouth and then swallow? Can you describe the movement quality? How about the feeling of the glass in your hand and the water flowing into your mouth? Has the visual focus of the water now vanished, as the water travels to a hidden vessel? What takes over after vision? Is the water cold? Are there smells, tastes, or sounds assisting you to engineer this performance? How do you coordinate your breathing with this flow of water in your body? There are countless minutiae to detail this "simple" performance. As an insider to this ritual, which aspects do *you* believe are *essential* to impart, in order to convey the vital core of the tradition?

Nearly every task we engage in is multisensory. The next time you take part in the water ritual, notice how your observation of this act has transformed simply because you are thoughtfully considering it. Also, the (self-)conscious "thinking through" of the process might change your ritual precisely because you are aware of the observation process. Participation informs and makes conscious concepts of performance, and, should you write a detailed description of the process, most likely many unconscious aspects would surface. Participation also reinforces the practice of the enactment within the body, solidifying the memory and embodiment of the act.

If you were to compare your ritual experience with a friend, undoubtedly it would differ, partially because you drink water differently but also because each of you experiences the grand event differently, notices particular characteristics, or makes contrasting assumptions regarding what is necessary to convey the essence of the ritual. Each person's account depends on their perspective, and is informed by their past experiences, their enculturated sensual orientation.

A clear and detailed description of even a simple experience is endless. My point here is that conveying lived experience is challenging, particularly if it is a performance practice you "know" in your body but do not regularly transmit to someone else—either through demonstration or through writing. This has been one of my fascinations in writing about dance transmission. Originally when I set out to conduct research, I asked dancers how they learn or how they know a particular movement. They rarely responded with more than a handful of words, such as—"I follow" (in lessons), "I watch," "I listen," or, taking my hand, "let me show you." The truth is, *I* didn't know how I embodied the art, which is why I stubbornly embraced the topic. Since I danced for thirty years prior to considering this question, I needed to take the stance of an ethnographer, collect "data," and traverse the analytical space between my embodied knowledge and collected field data to find the essence of the dance transmission.

Hopefully, this orientation reveals the challenges of ethnographic and artistic sensibilities. One of my concerns in the process of conducting fieldwork, analyzing the "data," and writing has been to understand the essential elements I believed needed to be imparted to convey concepts of transmission and the embodiment of art. I have been fascinated by what sensory modes different people privilege in the transmission of their art or within their discipline of choice. Their/my sensual orientation influences the end product. Through fieldwork I came to understand that we inhabit very different worlds.

the reticent composer

Backstory and Overview

Exploring sounds I could make with my mouth *in private* has been a preoccupation since I was small. My earliest memories of the preoccupation take me back to the age of six. Ask my sister, and she will recount car rides with my incessant (no doubt annoying) backseat experimentations often uttered into a crevice in the vinyl seat, both hands cupped along the jaw to create a passage between mouth and ear.

Later I would discover whole communities with thriving mouth music, doo-wop, Scottish *puirt à beul*, beatboxing, and Inuit *katajjaq*, to name only a few. Most recently I have participated in Deep Listening improvisations that require participants to plug their ears with their fingers or earplugs to listen to one's inner body soundings.

"the reticent composer" invites participants to compose a one-minute piece. The hitch—the piece is "performed" with the ears plugged so that all sounds produced resound *inside* one's head. I assigned "the reticent composer" to a large class of nonmusicians and learned how pleasurable a release the engagement was for many, particularly the shy participants. The playful nature of the challenge encouraged everyone to compose. To my surprise, extroverts and introverts enthusiastically contributed to the post-performance discussions.

Preparation (minimal)

Leaders need to prepare a simple example composition to demonstrate for their group. The compositions can be created on the fly, within class time, or as a take-home assignment.

Depending on the leader's context and aims for the group, simple earplugs may be purchased and distributed. Should one decide to use earplugs, hands are freed up to tap on the cranium or lips and so on. They are not necessary, however. See below for an example to provide the group.

Recipe

OPENING ANNOUNCEMENT

This week everyone will compose a one-minute piece for everyone to perform. The challenge: your piece will be created and performed entirely inside your head! Our craniums will become the concert halls.

STEPS

1. Cover your ears, either with your fingers, palms, or earplugs, to literally discover the sounds inside your head while exploring and developing a vocabulary of sounds you can make.
2. Be creative! For example, what kinds of sounds resound when you breathe, blink, growl, purr, make plosive lip pops, or rub your tongue along your upper teeth, to name only a few techniques.
3. After finding a sonic vocabulary that you like, how might you arrange the sounds to shape and compose time? How can you transition between the various techniques? Are there pragmatic aspects to segue from one sound to the next? Do you have specific directions? Would you like the performer to improvise? If so, to what degree? And what directions might you provide for realizing the improvisation?
4. Write down the instructions in a way you find suits your particular piece.
5. Be sure to name your piece.
6. Exchange pieces with the others in the group and perform all pieces.
7. Discuss.

Note to Leader

Providing an example helps enormously! I always write a simple piece on the whiteboard and ask everyone to perform it on the spot. At this point, less is more, so participants are encouraged to explore the sonic landscapes (literally) in their own heads.

It can be as simple as this:

1. Inhale deeply and exhale slowly, making an "S" sound. Pause for silence.
2. Repeat #1 but alter the "S" sounds by moving the lips differently (try moving the lips as in "wee o wee o").
3. Inhale, then while exhaling alternate between plosive "P" and "K" sounds until you are out of air.
4. Inhale, and then while exhaling flutter the lips (as in a raspberry). Pause.
5. Drum fingers lightly anywhere on your skull while also moving the tongue along the upper teeth. Pause.
6. Coda: blow out strongly, as if you are blowing out a candle.

Post-Exercise Discussion Topics

Sounds inside the body! The cranium as an instrument. Discovering that playful exploration fosters a wealth of diverse sounds.

How to choose the order of sounds to create a "composition"? What is the difference between composition and improvisation? Questions concerning time, specifically the feel of time passing—some find the one-minute duration passes quickly, others not.

Improvisation and composition.

Notating a piece.

What is a "performance" that is enacted by one person for themself?

How can we examine differences of the "performance," as each person's cranium, body, and experience is different?

Sensory Studies and Fieldwork

Sensory studies folks may find the idea of exploring one's inner realm interesting. Often ethnographers focus on what's "out there" in the world, outside of the body. Here, one's inner landscape is the world to be explored. The body *is* the field site. Reflexivity is key.

Creativity

I have found that the playful, unique challenge of creating a piece that is private and then "shared" for a private audience stirs participants up in interesting ways. They ask a lot of questions, some quite profound. Everyone smiles.

Clay in Space

Overview

The sensuous nature of working with clay can be engrossing. Fingers squishing, twisting, pushing, and rolling the clay provide a tactile encounter that magnifies relationships between embodied knowledge, intuition, and creativity. Clay allows for "thinking" fingers to playfully sculpt as one shapes and reshapes the amorphous blob. I stress the value in "mindlessly exploring" the nature of the clay. In so doing we explore the nature of our embodied knowledge and intelligence. No matter whether individuals have a set idea of what they will make before starting, or whether they jump in and start playing with the clay, there is always a need to work with the clay to see if *it suggests* or demands a different outcome in form. Materials speak. Noticing the properties and qualities of clay and exploring its material limitations can further new, embodied understandings. While reshaping an amorphous medium with our hands, we have an opportunity to fluidly imagine forms through direct sensory "thinking." While creating clay forms, participants are invited to imagine a setting for their clay objects and then to stage the clay in the context.

The recipe also has a variation that involves trading a story with another participant and then using some aspect of the story as an inspiration for the clay and scene.

Preparation (moderate)

Ingredients needed: clay, paper, and a marker. Optional: bamboo skewers (as tools or connectors). I often bring wet paper towels for hand and desk cleanup.

I suggest using plasticine modeling clay or homemade play-dough (a search online will provide many simple recipes). Each participant will receive

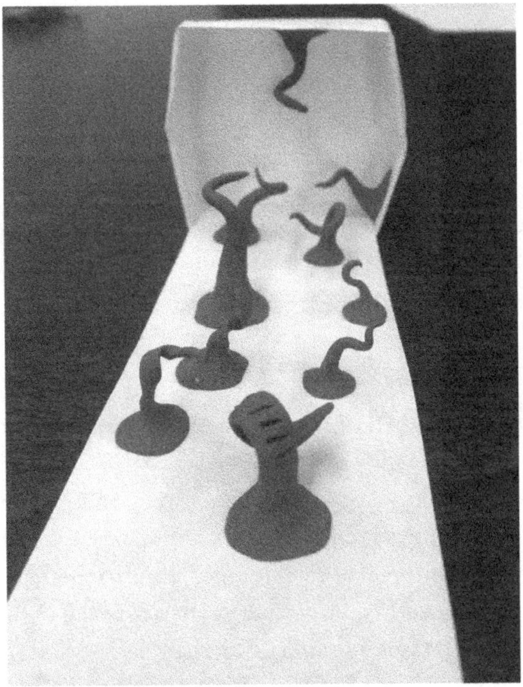

FIGURE 1. "Clay in Space": creation by Katie Boyd.

only a small wedge of clay, less than a ping-pong-ball-size hunk of clay. I find card stock paper works best. Photocopy paper can work, but I have found it is a bit flimsy for our purposes.

Recipe

OPENING ANNOUNCEMENT

Today everyone will receive a ball of clay and paper. Please have your journals nearby so you can take notes. The clay is for exploring and letting the clay suggest its shape. The paper will be used to construct a setting for your clay object. In a way, you are building a diorama.

STEPS

1. Exploring stage: When you receive your clay, take the first few minutes to explore its qualities—its firmness, its squishiness, and how much effort is necessary to knead it or roll it into a log, for example. I'm asking you to explore and play. Let the sensory exploration allow the clay to inform you, through the senses, of the shapes it can make and hold. Take three to ten minutes.
2. Now that you have explored and warmed up your clay, create an object, real or abstract, that you will later stage in a context. You can divide the clay into several objects if you like. Periodically jot down ideas for contexts in your journal. Take ten to twenty minutes to create your object.
3. You will create a context or stage set for your object with the paper. Draw on the paper with the markers provided. For example, you might fold the paper in half and create a stage set for the object, or curve the paper so the backdrop establishes more of a surrounding context, or fold the paper to simulate stairs.
4. Bring out your journals and freewrite, using your diorama as your own prompt.
5. Discuss.

Variation

Originally, I offered this recipe as "Clay Me a Story." The recipe is the same as "Clay in Space" except the group is divided into pairs. Participants describe a scene or environment, real or imagined, to their partners. The description can be in the form of a story. Participants then proceed with the steps provided above but build their diorama using their partner's scene as a prompt. The clay scene does not need to accurately represent their partner's story but is inspired in some way by it.

For example, in the clay diorama pictured, Katie Boyd's partner described a cave-like environment. Katie wrote,

> I interpreted the cave as the inside of the body, so when I was given the clay, I made a scene where there were curved figures farther back, and as they got closer to the viewer, they became flatter, more like DNA strands. Then, at the very front, I made a few strands with more detail, so you could see the recognizable double helix and ladder shape. The process was interesting, because I am used to working with pottery clay, not the modeling clay provided, so I had to use a different technique for making shapes. . . .
>
> It was interesting to listen to what the other groups were describing, and then to see what they made out of it. There were very interesting interpretations of the scenes. I think this could be because the scene had to go through many different forms before its final form. The first form would be the describer's experience that made the memory. The second form would be how they described it to the other person, and how much detail they went into, or how much they left out. (excerpted by permission)

Note to Leader

Sometimes I provide a theme for the group as a jumping-off point, especially if participants appear lost. Themes range from abstract shapes, fantastic monsters, and underwater creatures to furniture, rockets, birds, or trees.

While seemingly simple, I want to stress how deeply insightful participants find the exploration. The notion of tapping embodied knowledge and consciousness via the intelligent body through direct interaction with clay can shift a simple exploration into a profound realm of discovery.

Post-Exercise Discussion Topics

The joy of playing with clay and how it encourages relaxation and "zoning out."

Context-related themes.

Planning (and not planning) ahead: "I knew exactly what I wanted to make, then the clay couldn't stand up to my expectation" versus "I had no idea of what to make, but I'm happy with my creature. I've never made something like this before."

Sensory Studies and Fieldwork

The tactile interaction with clay reveals a good deal of embodied information. Participants grasp how the body "knows" and quickly realize how interacting with objects in their daily lives is also a relationship, an orientation of one's self to environment. When conducting fieldwork, sensory awareness needs to reach beyond dialogue, beyond only seeing or hearing, to include touch and other modalities.

Creativity

The enjoyment of working with clay, "listening" to what the clay suggests, has the mysterious power to calm and encourage creative intuition stemming from sensational knowledge. Working with clay has the potential to expand participants' vocabulary. I say "has the potential to" because participants will fall into habits unless they are fully encouraged to play and explore. Otherwise, the "same old" friends will appear, such as SpongeBob SquarePants, Mickey Mouse, a cube, a braid, and so on.

Shifting Point of View

Backstory and Overview

The experience of living with a bird, a small cockatoo (specifically, *Cacatua goffiniana*), for over thirty years fuels my curiosity about transmission and sensory translation. Beakie, the cockatoo, reminds me each day that we live in different sensory worlds, while at the same time we share the particulars of our own communication and environment. Her ability to sense details, time, ordering of events, patterns of sense, shapes, and sonic and visual minutiae continues to astound me. Don't get me wrong; she can be annoying, as cockatoos are smart and energetic and do their best to push boundaries! However, I believe many of our miscommunications rest on sensory misfires, meaning that Beakie insists something exists and I don't perceive it, or I have a project in mind for us and yet when I attempt to coordinate the project, our differences emerge. While sensory intelligence may be extremely diverse across species, my relationship with Beakie helps me to recognize that different sensory worlds exist. I often introduce this recipe with a story about Beakie to clarify the difficulties of "interpretation" of the senses and the idea of a shifting perspective. I encourage leaders to provide a personal story that helps the participants not only understand the prompt but also get to know you.

The notion of one's "point of view" gestures to a paradox, that we cannot assume that what one experiences is the same as someone else's experience. The conundrum offers insights into language as well. For example, notice how the English language emphasizes visual referents: "point of *view*" or "do you *see* what I mean?" or "*seeing* is believing," to point out only a few. I asked composer Pauline Oliveros, who loved ear references, how we might translate "point of view" for sound, and she grinned and replied, "How about 'field of sound'?" Our conversation made me realize that we could conceivably designate a different "point of view" reference to denote each sensory modality. In the long run, I believe an awareness of how language points to a culture's sensory weighting provides enough insights, and we need not reinvent our sensory-rich language.

The exploration provides an opportunity to engage with a wide range of sensory modalities to emphasize that sensory qualities are experienced on a continuum and as relational experiences. Because sensory experiences can be quite evocative, metaphors are particularly effective. I do not point out any of these observations prior to a group exploration, however. Instead, I wait for the post-exploration discussion to ensue, highlight them when they arise, or tease out the issues through inquiry.

A very creative piece, "The Size of Your Misconceptions" by Edlyn Terrazas, was written using the "Shifting Point of View" prompt and can be found in the "Resources" chapter at the close of the book.

Preparation (none)

"Shifting Point of View" can be workshopped on the spot or given to a group as a take-home project. The only preparation needed is for the leader to have a personal story to present.

Recipe (in Three Parts)

To leader: For three weeks in a row I assign the following perspective challenges. Of course, you are welcome to adapt the recipe.

OPENING ANNOUNCEMENT

Consider someone's or something's perspective or point of view for this week's prompt. You are encouraged to explore any sensory modality. Please interpret the challenge prompt in any way you would like. Should you have any concerns, however, do not hesitate to ask.

Part A: Week 1 challenge

Prompt: small and/or low.

STEPS

1a. As a take-home project, create—write, build, perform, photograph, make—something from a small *and/or* low perspective. The perspective needs to be from that being's or object's perspective, in a real or imagined sense. Feel free to incorporate a metaphoric perspective if that speaks to you.

1b. Written assignment (two pages): In addition to the creative project, write a paper reflecting upon your creative process, including how you selected the point of view to tackle and how you proceeded to develop and realize the creative project.

2. On the due date, bring in your creation and present it to our group. (*Note to leader*: if the creative project is a written one, you might want to limit how many pages are presented. I often ask for a two- or three-page excerpt if the piece is very long.)
3. Discuss as a group.

Part B: Week 2 challenge

Prompt: big and/or tall.

STEPS

1. Repeat #1–3 above with the challenge 2 prompt.

Part C: Week 3 challenge

Prompt: inside and/or outside.

STEPS

1. Repeat #1–3 above with the challenge 3 prompt.

Note to Leader

Depending on the group and focus of the workshop, including information about the senses and awareness can help to contextualize the exploration. I often run the first challenge without any mention of what themes might arise so that the participants have an opportunity for discovering their own themes. Following the challenge 1 group presentations and discussion, I will often talk about "point of view" and the senses paradox prior to assigning challenge 2.

For some workshops I emphasize that the project (outcome), while important, is not entirely the point of the challenge. The real outcome is how they arrived at their decision and what they realized in the process of creating it.

Post-Exercise Discussion Topics

"Point of view" is relative!

Metaphors about perspective reveal a lot about one's identity, experiences, and (cultural) background.

The attempt to shift one's point of view is challenging and increases empathy.

Sensory Studies and Fieldwork

The "Shifting Point of View" exploration lends itself well to sensory fieldwork workshops. While the exploration may appear simple at first glance, don't underestimate it. Participants always return with fascinating sensory stories about how they approached the challenge and the outcome of their projects. Participants discover quickly that their sensory perspectives are their own. Also, sensory perspectives are relative and relational; for example, "big" *relative to what or whom*?

Creativity

I have been surprised by the wealth of creative projects that arrive on the first day. When the medium is left open-ended, participants feel the freedom to write a poem, sculpt, take photographs, and so on. They do struggle with writing about their process, but that very struggle can be quite moving and mind-blowing.

Bonding in Parallel, a Writing Collaboration

Overview

Synergy mixed with collaboration, chance, and openness brews an interesting recipe to support compassionate empathy. The following recipe may appear simple, yet don't miss the opportunity to dig deeper, to realize that the recipe offers not only an interesting window to observe a relationship of words but more importantly a window into the relationship of authors in collaboration. Because two authors are writing in parallel, the collaboration arises from juxtapositions, from closeness. The discussion that emerges may be the most productive aspect of this recipe.

"Bonding in Parallel" works well as a distant collaboration (done in real-time on the phone or via another online platform). An example, "Excavating Time," by Lorelei Wagner and myself, can be found in the "Resources" chapter at the close of the book.

Preparation (little to none)

Each partner needs to select an object to write about. It does not need to be special, just one that fosters twenty minutes of freewriting. Create two columns in an electronic document for the partners to use. See "Excavating Time" collaboration included in the "Resources" section for a template example.

Recipe

OPENING ANNOUNCEMENT

Each person selects any object in the room to use as a prompt. The aim is to be inspired by the object, *yet not name or disclose what the object is*. In a sense, writers are writing around the object.

STEPS

1. For a group: pair up and decide which column of the page you will write in. Online or via phone: contact your partner to say hello and ask whether they are ready. Explain the recipe (see "Opening Announcement" above), say goodbye, and begin writing.
2. Freewrite for approximately ten to twenty minutes, writing in your own column, in any style. My preference is to keep the writing to one page. Reminder: Do not disclose what the object is.

3. Contact each other again and share documents, cutting and pasting the partner's text into the parallel column.
4. After you have exchanged texts, also share the identity of your objects. If you are conducting the recipe distantly, take a photo of the object and share it with your partner.
5. Have a discussion with your partner first (then as a group), noticing any parallels, correspondences, synergies, spacing, patterns, repeating themes, flow, shapes in text, and so on. Does the piece need a title? If so, how will you collaboratively create one?
6. Optional: As you and your partner discuss your collaboration, consider highlighting a word or single line in boldface in each column.

Note to Leader

When writing "Excavating Time," my writing partner placed one line in her text in boldface. The simple idea encouraged me to do the same to a single line and to include the optional step #6 above. We noted how the boldfaced lines enhanced the connection between the two columns. During a different workshop I saw how participants were inspired to use boldface on several lines on each side. Participants felt that these highlighted texts became a third text, one that is shared by both sides yet also hovers over each side.

As I mentioned in the introduction, collaboration and improvisation with others can reveal a number of personal tendencies, specifically related to social skills and communication. Because collaborators work only on their own column in "Bonding in Parallel," participants can retain their style and agency, leaving the collaborative aspect to the juxtaposition and discussion. This recipe can prime more deeply integrated, collaborative work. Discussion between the collaborators (and then as a group) can raise interesting observations and opinions about collaborative process. I ask everyone to stay alert to their ways of communicating during this period of sharing, as collaborations reveal interesting social tendencies. I point out that noticing one's own impulses, or even biases, *enables freedom.*

Post-Exercise Discussion Topics

Participants notice how the juxtaposition of texts in parallel offers a different reading of both texts. They are often startled by how many correlations appear. Empathy rolls in.

Sensory Studies and Fieldwork

Participants in sensory studies workshops find that observing and writing about an object for twenty minutes compels them to be attentive to the sensory qualities in their environment. The observation leads them to notice subtle aspects they might have overlooked. Conversations about an object while in the field or during an interview can often kickstart interesting stories.

Creativity

"Bonding in Parallel" offers a great testing ground for collaboration and, even better, for observing the nature of collaboration (see "Note to Leader" above). Relationships and bonding emerge through a shared perspective of the parallel creation, through how the piece came to be, and through the conversation about the collaboration. In the group discussion there is an opportunity for pairs to comment on how the two columns related, or did not, and how the juxtaposition of the columns altered their perspective.

Scent of Time

Backstory and Overview

Ten years ago, I was crossing a street in New York City and had an arresting experience. I found myself transported to another time and place . . . as a five-year-old in Tokyo walking home from school. Back in NYC, I realized that the smell of freshly baked bread permeating the air elicited a childhood memory that dramatically flung me back to a very particular time and place. The sensory experience was vivid on both sides of the time shift. I could visualize, feel, and smell the very location decades past. However, as my olfactory experience of the baked bread in New York faded while crossing the street, so did the memory. Have you ever been whisked away by a scent memory, including memories of particular people, foods, and locations?

"Scent of Time" draws attention to our sense of smell as a time-based experience on several levels. Time can be observed at the moment one notices a scent and how it dissipates. The encounter affords an examination of the ephemeral experience of smell, as airborne scent particles disperse at different rates depending on the context (weather, for example), and on the properties of what is bringing about the scent. Your physical capacity to smell and your awareness of odors certainly affects your experience. An olfactory experience can prompt imprinted memories and associations from the past, providing us with physical recollections from our scent vocabulary. The memories, summoned by smell, are uniquely tied to one's personal experiences, making them ideal candidates for creative prompts.

"Scent of Time" works well with groups of fewer than twenty participants (unless you have an assistant). Participants are introduced to a natural scent, such as a lemon, while their eyes are closed. Afterward they are asked to reflect on the experience and to write or draw their observations or stories.

If appropriate, I combine the exercise with a reading about dogs' refined sense of smell. Psychologist Alexandra Horowitz's research reports that dogs' heightened sense of smell conveys the passage of time. She has written numerous articles and books on the subject (see Horowitz 2016, 2017).

A nostalgic excerpt from Abdullah Alshehri's moving story "Lemon Memories" can be found in the "Resources" chapter at the close of the book.

Preparation (moderate)

I often use a lemon for the scent but have also used fresh rosemary or cinnamon sticks. I stay away from bottled essences. Prior to the workshop, I place slices of lemon, squeezed a bit, in an opaque plastic cup. The cup prevents the participants from accidentally viewing the scent source and also concentrates the smell inside it. It is helpful to have an assistant so you can prepare two cups and traverse the room more quickly.

Recipe

OPENING ANNOUNCEMENT

Today we explore the sense of smell. I will visit each participant and hold a cup with a natural scent near your nose. Because you will have your eyes closed, when I come by I'll say, "Ready, [*name of student*]?" or tap you on the shoulder when I arrive to offer you the scent.

Once everyone has had a chance to smell it, I will inform the group so everyone can open their eyes and begin freewriting/drawing. I urge everyone not to talk during the session.

STEPS

1. Take out a notebook and pen and place them near you.
2. Sit in your seat comfortably. Relax and close your eyes. Breathe naturally and settle into observation mode.
3. When I come to you with the scent, breathe naturally and notice any reactions in your body or thoughts. (*Note to leader*: I tend not to mention specifics of participants' potential reactions, such as salivating or childhood memories, so that these words do not become suggestions or even get interpreted as "getting it right.")
4. (*After everyone has had a chance to smell the object*:) Open your eyes. Please do not talk. Freewrite/draw for ten to fifteen minutes.
5. If anyone needs a "re-smelling" of the object for follow-up, hold up your hand.
6. Discuss and/or share passages of writing or drawings.

Note to Leader

It is common for participants not to identify the scent source. Some even become frustrated. I always reassure them that the point of the exercise is not to correctly identify the source but to broaden our awareness of how our sense of smell precipitates connections between the body and memory, questions about time, and the relationship of smell to other sensory modalities.

Post-Exercise Discussion Topics

Smell as a time-based experience and how the experience of a scent may change over time.

Curiosity about dissipation or "disappearance" of a scent.

Relationship between taste and smell.

How might smell be connected to safety, eating and flavor, appetite, tracking, memories and associations, and other sensory modalities? In participants' writings and discussions, color is often mentioned, and we have fascinating discussions about synesthesia.

Sensory Studies and Fieldwork

As a sensory fieldwork exercise, "Scent of Time" usually reveals a range of topics to examine, such as sensory display over time, dispersion of particles, presence, associations or overlapping of other sensory modalities, memory, tracking, social and cultural predilections (or tolerance) for different scents, scent references that can be generational or gender based, and commercials for scents, to name only a few.

Creativity

"Scent of Time" works well as a sensory prompt for creative work. Memories and associations pop up quickly, and participants will generally cry out for a time extension to write or draw.

Story Exchange

Overview

Listening and observing people during interviews is an important research method for ethnographers. Catching the words are important. However, *how* the stories are told can reveal so much more about the storyteller and context, including pacing, gestures, facial expression, eye gaze, tone of voice, and loudness, to name a few examples.

"Story Exchange" explores the art of listening and observing a partner tell a story. The key is that the listener is not permitted to interrupt. Just listen and observe.

Workshops developed for listening to spoken word are certainly not unusual. There are many exercises that can be used in a workshop for developing presence and listening to a partner's spoken word. I offer "Story Exchange" for its simplicity, centering, and fostering of compassion. Try it out and make it your own. See the "Note to Leader" section below for other insights.

Preparation (minimal)

Prepare a sensory-rich, engaging story of your own to tell the group (one to five minutes). I strongly discourage reading a story, as you will be asking everyone to come up with a story on the spot.

Recipe

I begin the session by greeting everyone. Then I wait in silence, sometimes with eyes closed, for everyone to settle. My lack of interaction after the initial greeting always raises their curiosity and sets the stage for storytelling. Once the class is still, I begin. The story serves as an example of what I will be asking them to share. My storytelling often reveals my own vulnerabilities and also the humanity of exchanging stories. Because of the kinds of classes and workshops that I offer, the stories range from tales of a scar to a childhood "realization" story or a sensory-rich story stemming from a simple experience (some examples: walking on a beach barefoot, a new food experience, an encounter during travel).

OPENING ANNOUNCEMENT

I just shared a short personal story with you. Today everyone will have a chance to tell a story and listen to a story with someone in our group. However, this exploration requires that the designated listeners not speak a word until the story has concluded.

In everyday communication we are accustomed to asking questions or interrupting. I ask that the listeners relax and enjoy absorbing and observing the storytellers but also observe their own tendencies for interaction. *We need to realize that by interrupting, we actively change the timeline of our partner's story flow.*

STEPS

1. First, let's divide into pairs. (If there is an odd number, a group of three will work.) Please have your notebooks and pens nearby.
2. Everyone take a moment to recall an experience that you can tell your partner as a story. The story should take approximately five minutes. A personal experience that provides nuance works well. After you know what your story will be, decide which partner will share first. Partner A is the storyteller and Partner B the listener. However, the roles will switch.

   (*Important note to leader:* Tell participants that their story *might be* shared with the entire group. You don't want a participant to be placed in an uncomfortable situation because a personal story was shared.)
3. Partner A, the storyteller: tell your story.

   Partner B, the listener: listen intently. *No speaking!* This is important. You *can* make sounds of acknowledgment, such as "Uh huh" or "Mmmm," *but speak no words*. Occasional gestures, smiles/frowns, or nods are fine, but keep at a minimum. Notice everything about how the story is being told: pauses, silence, loudness or softness, the quality of the speaker's voice, movements, facial expressions, and so on.

4. I will be the timekeeper and say "one more minute" around four minutes in, then I will ring a bell at five minutes. (*To leader*: I'm flexible here and allow for a few minutes for the stories to complete. I often ask, "Need another minute?")
5. Both partners jot a few thoughts in their journals about their experience. For example, they can write about the process, including what they noticed about themselves, observations of their partner, and notes about the story itself (two to three minutes).
6. Switch roles (repeating steps #3–5).
7. Discuss.

Three Variations

1. Ask participants to retell their partner's story *in brief* to the whole class.
2. Include a theme as a prompt for the story. Themes tend to unify the class so that individual stories, as diverse as they might be, emerge as variations on a theme of being human. Themes I often incorporate: the story of a trip; the story of an animal friend; the story of a eureka moment. When using a theme, the story I share to open class introduces the theme.
3. Participants take some aspect of their partner's story to use as a prompt and write/draw a new piece. If there is no time, this variation can be assigned for the next class.

Note to Leader

As noted above, it is important to tell participants that their story might be shared with the class. An announcement about sharing may change participants' choice of what story to tell. They may feel comfortable telling a story to their partner but not to the entire group.

Post-Exercise Discussion Topics

Participants consistently voice their difficulties about being quiet and not responding or interrupting the presenter when taking on the listener role—primarily their inability to remain silent. Because it feels unnatural not to respond, a number of realizations surfaced in the participants' reports: "I noticed more about the story and my partner," "I had no idea how much I fidget," "I was so self-conscious," "I honestly didn't realize how often I interrupt . . . this was hard!"

Participants noticed the challenges of observing nonverbal aspects of storytelling.

Sensory Studies and Fieldwork

Groups employing "Story Exchange" will find that the exploration works well as a practice interview session. When transcribing interview tapes, ethnographers soon realize how often they change the course of an interview by interrupting, steering, commenting, or gesturing. In addition, the recipe highlights the importance of noting nonverbal expressivity as a communication of embodied knowledge, as well as details of the interview context.

Creativity

"Story Exchange" encourages participants in a creative workshop to learn from another person, be focused on the interaction, and deepen empathy. I hope groups exploring creative work will take on Variation #3, in which listeners reflect on the story they heard and then incorporate some aspect of it as a prompt for a new story that is entirely their own. The exchange encourages bonding in the class and a positive exchange.

Pareidolia Crawl

Overview

Have you ever seen an image appear in an abstract design? The man or rabbit in the moon? Perhaps as a child gazing up at the sky you noticed that the clouds took on whimsical forms gliding along—dragons, animals, faces, rocket ships? Did you share what you saw by describing it, narrating, pointing, and even creating a story line? You are not alone. I believe most of us have enjoyed the ever-changing shapes of clouds.

The phenomenon of seeing images emerge from amorphous shapes is called pareidolia. Specifically, pareidolia is when a person recognizes pattern and meaning in ambiguous forms or random stimuli, such as seeing the Virgin Mary in a tortilla, faces in landscapes, creatures in clouds, or faces in a Rorschach inkblot, to name a few. Humans have a particular tendency to see faces appear in abstract designs or common objects, such as electrical sockets, rocks, or woodgrain (Bednarik 2016). One can imagine why experiencing such a phenomenon would foster worldviews or spiritual passions in some cultural contexts. Look up "pareidolia" in an online image search to view a variety of interesting visual examples. There are other sensory pareidolia, such as auditory and tactile.

"Pareidolia Crawl" is a geological hunt for inspiration by viewing a satellite image of the earth (via Google Earth or another search engine). Participants do not need to encounter a pareidolia phenomenon. However, often abstract images prompt a "making sense" of what one sees.

This recipe works well as an online, distant, or asynchronous group challenge.

Preparation (minimal)

Using the satellite view on Google Earth (or another search engine), locate an abstract aerial view that you can project for the group. The point here is to project an image that is as abstract as possible. It is best if the map does not contain any text or identifiable features that would be distracting. Turn off locators and zoom the frame out, so that roads and land markers do not appear.

Try a Google Earth search of "Mohave County, AZ," then zoom in and move the image until an abstract region of interesting land appears.

If incorporating "Pareidolia Crawl" into a workshop that is delivered online, I suggest either providing a URL, asking participants to find a satellite view that inspires them, or distributing a screenshot for everyone to work with. In a pinch, leaders can photograph abstract scenes such as coral, rocks, or landscape and adapt the opening announcement.

Recipe

OPENING ANNOUNCEMENT

Today we will look at an abstract aerial view of the earth to find inspiration for making or writing. The actual location is not important. Because the satellite view displays an aerial map that is abstract, there are quite a number of ways you can respond to the prompt.

STEPS

1. Everyone look at the aerial view projected (or displayed as an image). Give yourself at least five minutes to take in the image without responding. Allow your imagination to wander and settle.
2. Jot down a few words and/or draw in your notebook. If an idea for a narrative or a drawing comes to you, feel free to dive in.

3. The aerial view image is your prompt. Please freewrite or draw for the next fifteen minutes. (*To leader*: After about fifteen or twenty minutes, ask the group if they need another minute.)
4. Discuss and/or share passages of writing or drawings.

Note to Leader

I never talk about pareidolia prior to the activity. However, in almost every workshop someone writes about how an image of a face or shape appeared. During the discussion, if no one talks about seeing an image appear, I will ask, "Did anyone find that some of the abstract shapes in the aerial view appeared like something familiar?" Of course, some participants may feel uncomfortable about announcing to a group that they had such an experience. Therefore, during the discussion I talk about the phenomenon of pareidolia and how the human tendency to see forms in abstract designs is common. I use the example of clouds and woodgrain, and then everyone is on board.

Post-Exercise Discussion Topics

Regarding pareidolia, see the "Note to Leader" section above. Depending on the group and how much time there is, sometimes I give a presentation on pareidolia and provide a number of examples.

The topic of maps and journeys often comes up. Participants might create stories that take place in the landscape provided.

A few days or weeks after the workshop, participants might report that they notice the abstract textures around them and playfully note whether any images pop up.

Sensory Studies and Fieldwork

For groups doing fieldwork, the practice of viewing images from a variety of perspectives can be valuable. Some cultures may hold deep considerations about how something looks or appears to them that may not "make sense" to the ethnographer. Also, the notion of pareidolia tends to throw a monkey wrench into the mix, encouraging a questioning of reality and a curiosity for how different people make sense of the world they populate.

Creativity

The whimsical quality of the assignment can open up participants' viewing of abstract textures. Some find the exercise relaxing, especially if ample time is provided for the group to ponder the aerial view. I believe the far-reaching effects on heightening awareness and incorporating that sensibility into participants' everyday life is valuable.

Sound, Moving

Backstory and Overview

Over the last fifteen years I have been observing bats' flight patterns at nightfall, mesmerized by how they swoop swiftly around the field and pond near my house. They skim the water, elegantly dart between trees, and head skyward above the canopy. I've never witnessed a fatal collision. Echolocation rocks!

"Sound, Moving" aims to heighten attendance to auditory spatial sensibilities—particularly the movement of sound, sound qualities (timbre), and the arc of a "piece." The exploration is simple. The leader asks everyone to close their eyes and then listen to abstract sounds that the leader creates behind them. Curiously, "Sound, Moving" pairs well with "Pareidolia Crawl," as the sounds can often prompt imagined sound worlds similar to aural pareidolia.

Depending on the aims of the workshop, "Sound, Moving" can be used to stage thick description of sound (for sensory studies, for example) or to prompt creative imagination through writing, drawing, or other medium.

Preparation (minimal)

Prior to the workshop, find a few objects that produce a variety of timbres. Refrain from using musical instruments; I prefer selecting only one or two objects and then challenge myself to explore the range of sounds I can discover over time. For example, how many timbral qualities can you elicit from a plastic bag, bubble wrap, a paper cup, a bouquet of cable zip ties (surprisingly, this evokes a wide variety of stimulating sounds), a toothbrush rubbed on textured cardboard? You get the idea. Vary the sounds, the lack of sound, where the sound is coming from, and the movement of the sound through space. Let the group be bats. Note: When I have a large group, I set up the classroom prior to the participants' arrival (see step #1 below).

Recipe

OPENING ANNOUNCEMENT

Today we are exploring the sense of sound and movement. You will be listening to approximately one minute of sound, followed by a session of writing and/or drawing.

The point is not to identify the object or sound but to merely listen and be open to how the sound unfurls. Since it is human to wonder what an unidentified sound is, the exercise is an interesting practice of noticing.

STEPS

1. Let's set up the classroom so everyone is facing one direction. Have your notebooks and pens nearby.
2. Everyone close your eyes so that sound can be your sensory focus. Relax and settle in.
3. Everyone breathe in. Breathe out. Listen. (*Leader:* Walking behind the group to shift the sound location, create a short sound world as a prompt for the group's listening practice, approximately one minute. The key is to move the sound object close and far, up and down, side to side. I always include a diversity of loud-to-quiet passages and silent pauses. At the close, pause for a few seconds to clarify that the listening period is completed.)
4. Without talking, go directly to your notebooks to write and/or draw for ten minutes.

Post-Exercise Discussion Topics

Participants note their struggles and yearning to identify the object (as a human trait) despite the request to resist.

Curiosity about how abstract sounds can prompt narratives. Some participants imagine an entire narrative from the sonic landscape, reflecting how the movement of sounds in time suggested a story. See "Pareidolia Crawl."

Sensory Studies and Fieldwork

For a sensory ethnography or fieldwork class, ask the group to focus on attending to and writing about the sonic details that they hear over time. Do the movements and sounds correspond to an event occurring in the space? Do they imply meaning to you? If the recipe is repeated several times over the course of a semester or workshop, do the participants notice that they are building a sonic movement vocabulary and awareness?

Creativity

I urge groups meeting for creative purposes to relax and let their curiosity fuel their imaginations during "Sound, Moving." In contrast to the sensory fieldwork focus, a group focused on creative, practice-based explorations might do better at allowing their inner narratives to flow versus endeavoring to identify the various sound objects.

Repeat That!

Backstory and Overview

Years ago, I was working on a line sketch for a drawing. My collaborator, noting my frustration with my first iteration, jumped in and encouraged me to rough sketch the *same scene* ten times. Although initially daunted by the sheer volume she requested, inspiration struck, and I returned a few days later with a notebook filled with over twenty versions. What started as a task became a curious challenge that I enjoy and have folded into my practice. Oddly, the practice of repeating a brush stroke in calligraphy or a musical or dance phrase in rehearsal has been so common in my vocabulary, but the idea of redrawing a sketch or rewriting a passage felt foreign. The rhythm of repeating became addictive, and in the process the practice was embodied and new developments enabled.

"Repeat That!" enhances other recipes, such as the "Sound, Moving" recipe. It can also be incorporated into nearly any of the explorations to generate and edit material. Participants are asked to write a draft, then start from scratch and write a fresh piece, then repeat a number of times (generally seven to ten iterations). Consider the exploration as "super-heroic sprinting" to encourage generating material and avoid overthinking. Participants often have embodied realizations while practicing the rhythms of repetition.

Preparation (little to none)

Because this recipe relies on complementing other recipes, leaders will need to consider what exercise, theme, or sensory modality to build upon.

Recipe

STEPS

1. *To leader:* Once the group has written for five to ten minutes after the "Sound, Moving" sound prompt (or a single word prompt; see "On the Go" chapter), announce: Everyone take the next twenty seconds to note where you were going with the draft. Write a few words to remind you where the piece might go, should you want to pick up where you left off.

After twenty seconds . . .

2. Everyone stop. Draw a line in your notebook and write the number 2. Start a completely new piece based on the same sonic prompt. This time you will have only three minutes to write, so start immediately!

To leader: Repeat #1 above at least seven times. I personally try to get up to ten repetitions, but seven consistently seems like a natural threshold.

Post-Exercise Discussion Topics

Participants often react with wide eyes, gasps, or plosive verbal outbursts after two or three iterations. For some, it seems they are questioning, in shock, or even protesting, "What . . . again?" But I cheer them on: "Come on, you CAN do this!"

Despite the squirming, the discussion afterward often reveals that the group generated a lot of material. Participants comment that they were writing (or drawing) so fast and so much that they had little time to ponder what to write. In other words, the multiple iterations urged them to write extemporaneously. The new material they generate can push them to new styles of writing and new material, and they exclaim, "I don't know where this (story) came from" or "I never knew I could write like this." I was delighted to see final papers that reflected an iterative style; for example, I received one with seven stanzas generated from each repetition.

Sensory Studies and Fieldwork

Rewriting a draft seven times or more develops an important practice that can be encouraged for taking fieldnotes or moving from fieldnotes to a larger text. The re-articulation of the same experience or idea encourages observation from multiple perspectives, to push for greater detail in the "thick description" vein, different material, different responses, and the idea that, over time, our perceptions of a context change. The ability to note change is valuable. The feeling of embodied rhythmic repetitions can raise one's sensory awareness of shifting perspectives as well as anticipation.

Creativity

As described in the "Backstory and Overview" section above, the fundamental notion of reworking an idea, a creative design, a written passage, or a musical or movement phrase is not new. One of the advantages of "Repeat That!" is that the practice generates a diversity of material. The repeating process exposes some interesting characteristics—that embodiment arises through repetition and that the *rhythms of practice* can become embodied in a potentially profound way.

Broad Strokes, Then Details

Overview

This recipe helps to frame large- to small-scale sensory qualities and to highlight prominent features from the vast array of sensory information from our environment at any given time. The recipe works well as an exercise for those working solo or in a group. Start simple. The simplicity of early observations leads to an awareness of details that reveal a staggering amount of sensory nuance. The recipe helps participants recognize awareness of different levels of attention and filtering ("inattentional blindness"; see Chabris and Simons 2010).

I tend to offer this exploration several times within one session. The first round is general, then the following iterations focus on one particular sensory modality. See below for alternate forms for notation (notebook versus laptop versus audio).

Preparation (minimal)

I encourage participants to go outdoors. If possible, I ask participants to select a familiar location. Following the first round, a secondary exploration in an unfamiliar location can be incorporated.

Recipe

STEPS

1. Settle yourself in a location of your choice: find a comfortable seat, lie down, or stand.
2. Take a few minutes to observe your surroundings. Absorb the scene around you.
3. Write "broad stroke" observations in your notebook. By "broad stroke" I mean the most general, large-scale observations possible. At this point, limit your jottings to three to five "broad strokes."

   Examples of five "broad strokes":
   - spring day outdoors in Central Park
   - sitting on a wooden park bench
   - chilly breeze, bright sun
   - people laughing, distant traffic
   - pigeons looking for handouts
4. Set notebook aside. Settle back into observation mode again, this time for at least ten minutes.
5. Write or draw the details *for each* of the first set of broad strokes. What other broad strokes might you add? Jot them down. Return to writing up the details of broad strokes.
6. Note sensory details. For each broad stroke, what specific sensory information informs you? Smells? Lighting? Movement? Timing? Atmosphere?
7. What sensory details repeat? If so, in what timescale? What sensory details are repeating? For example, does a particular sound repeat every twenty-five seconds? Does the sound correspond to a light, or to movement of someone or something?

   Noticing correspondence might supply insights into social and cultural concepts of form, structure, social norms, or unusual occurrences. Perhaps you noticed that a particular pattern appeared in the dirt road each morning, but that pattern was missing by the afternoon. In the Central Park scenario, perhaps you noticed people tended to pass by in waves corresponding to a traffic light or a subway exit.
8. Notice how some sensory details dissipate or even disappear (for example, perhaps the pigeons flew away).
9. Repeat and then repeat and then repeat.

Variation 1: Alternate Forms of Notation

Alternating between noting my observations via computer and recording them in a physical notebook can be interesting. I notice that different patterns arise simply because of the medium I use. Some participants like creating an audio file journal, dictating their observations into a recording device.

Variation 2: Mapping

Start with a few terse observations randomly across a page. Draw a circle around each observation. After the first round of broad stroke observations, add details having to do with each theme around its designated circle. The patterns that emerge resemble fractals or "mind maps," and I find that the different manner of display provides alternate perspectives on the scene.

Post-Exercise Discussion Topics

Questions that emerge tend to reveal insights about process. What do we attend to? How do we make choices of focus? What are larger frames (broad strokes)? What determines the granularity of sensory information and awareness? How do we filter information?

Sensory Studies and Fieldwork

For groups workshopping sensory ethnography or fieldwork projects, "Broad Strokes, Then Details" provides a flexible perspective that helps to map a large-scale view, then details. It demands a wide-angle view that shifts incrementally, telescopically. The recipe can offer a variety of insights into one's initial, cursory experience and emphasizes the additional insights gleaned when revisiting a scene with an increasingly granular perspective. The refocusing or recontextualizing of one's sensory field facilitates a shifting of frames and timescales that can be profound. One of the most valuable outcomes is a heightened awareness to sensory patterns that arise over time.

Creativity

The exploration of large to small frames of attention to a scene mirrors many compositional practices. For example, when drawing a duck, an initial sketch might consist of two ovals connected by a thin rectangle (body + head + neck). The details then emerge through adding legs and feet, feathers, beak, and so on. Noticing the abstract, larger structural form helps to focus one's attention to general structures first. The details can then be layered onto the basic structure. The recipe can also inspire creative flow by the simple adjustment of perspective and sensory awareness.

Sensory Focusing

Overview

How can we develop sensory awareness? How can such awareness help us to understand ourselves and others? How can we invite participants to investigate and explore different sensory experiences in workshops?

"Sensory Focusing" requires participants to go deeper, to find increasingly nuanced qualities of sense. Note that the recipe "Broad Strokes, Then Details" is similar to "Sensory Focusing," and you may opt to use one or the other or pair them up. I tend to use one earlier in the semester (or workshop) and the other a few weeks later. As usual, alter the recipe if you are using this as a personal exercise (outside of a group). This recipe works well as a personal practice.

Preparation (none)

Ask participants to bring an object that is very familiar to them, perhaps a favorite stone, or a key, or even a shoe. In a pinch, participants can use an object they already have with them, such as a wallet, a piece of jewelry, or a watch.

Recipe (in Two Parts)

OPENING ANNOUNCEMENT

Please bring out your objects and your notebooks (or a blank sheet of paper) and place the object where you can see it. If you have forgotten to bring one, find one that you are familiar with in your belongings.

Part A

STEPS

1. Five-minute visual observation: place your object on your desk or on another resting place where it will not move. For the next five minutes station yourself so that you can observe your object visually. Refrain from moving or touching the object, as this particular encounter is to narrow the focus on a single sensory modality first.
2. After the five minutes, turn away from the object or cover it so that you cannot see it, and take two minutes to *quickly jot down* as many visual observations as possible. Challenge your memory!
3. Return to viewing the object. What have you missed? At this point, take two more minutes to view the object and add more detailed observations to your earlier notebook jottings.

Part B

To leader: At this point you can decide if pairing up participants would be productive.

STEPS

1. After finishing Part A, trade objects with your partner (or, if the group is not paired up, with someone else in the group).
2. Repeat Part A.
3. Discuss your experiences and what you jotted down. Compare notes, observations, and experiences.

To leader: Questions to encourage discussion: What did you notice? Were the two experiences different? Ponder why your experiences were similar or different. What was left out? Included? Were your quick notes and jottings different? Were there differences in your observations, content, written voice, or form? Discuss as many details as possible.

If there is time and the workshop size appropriate, ask participants to share their thoughts and observations as well as those of their small group to everyone in the group. In other words, participants are sharing their meta-observations, or observations *of observations*!

Note to Leader

"Sensory Focusing" is written up as a visual observation, but I encourage tactile observations, if the setting is appropriate.

The time periods given are simply suggestions. I notice that each occasion I offer this exercise, the participants need different amounts of time to process. For this reason, I find that I can build an awareness of a particular group by observing them and being sensitive to their processing needs.

Post-Exercise Discussion Topics

While objects that are brought in may seem familiar to the participant, it is common for the familiarity to "blind" the participant of the nuances. The familiarity also holds personal memories or attachments that others may not be aware of. For example, one participant said, "I remember when my friend made me this bracelet. Each color has a significance." Of course, her workshop partner did not have this personal association and wrote a story about braiding hair.

Sensory Studies and Fieldwork

Observations during fieldwork differ greatly from person to person. Often it is the outsider who notices a continuum of sensory features, from large-scale frameworks to details. Acknowledging that each person experiences the world differently because of their past life experiences is valuable.

Creativity

If you use "Sensory Focusing" in creativity workshops, you will note that it expands everyone's awareness of their own sensory vocabulary and predilections. Noticing details about objects and people supports character development when writing a story or painting a scene.

Three Traces

Often the fading or absence of sensory information tantalizes the curiosity. Fascinated by the notion of a lingering sensory experience and how time might affect our perception and memory, I created three "Traces" recipes: "Traces, Presence," "Traces, Touch," and "Traces, Surface." These recipes are grouped together because all three address the often hidden or subtle essence of a sensory expression. Each sensory modality expresses (manifests) energy and existence over time differently. In addition, how (and if) we perceive the time-based essence, the lingering and fading, will be different depending on the context, who we are, and what we notice.

The "Traces" recipes dwell on a lingering, or *absence*, of sensory information. However, remnants of sense persist just enough to leave powerful clues—traces! We merely need to be aware, in time. (Regarding inexplicable sensory encounters in fieldwork, see Hahn [2017b].) Although each recipe targets one or two sensory modalities, in reality sensory experiences tend to overlap or gesture to another sensory modality in fascinating ways, as linkages of cognition and memory. A frailty of the senses and of our existence remains in the passing of time and experience.

Traces, Presence

Backstory and Overview

Many objects and living things leave traces—what I call sensory memory footprints. What lingers in our memory? Is it selective? Does the absence of the object leave a trace? If a parked car is moved after a light rain or snow flurries, it leaves a dry silhouette on the pavement—a clue that "something" existed there and left a trace. Admittedly, I normally took these negative spaces for granted, especially when the dry pavement was contextualized along a curb or parking lot. However, on a brisk walk in Cambridge, Massachusetts, I came upon an oddly shaped trace, stenciled by a light snowfall in the morning. I stopped to ponder the trace—a particularly curious, asymmetrical shape. The puzzling silhouette threw my imagination into overdrive, and I could almost watch my mind search through my vocabulary of objects. Human object recognition. I was mentally building an imagined object from the bottom up, like a 3D printer. There is no "Ah ha!" ending to my story, yet my active mind attempting to recreate a contour from a trace inspired a number of projects, including this exploration.

"Traces, Presence" conjures notions of presence, absence, memory, impression, palimpsest, erasure, and sensory awareness. An object is displayed and then removed, compelling everyone to rely on their sensory memory of the object, person, and context.

Preparation (moderate)

Prior to the workshop, select an object to display prominently. Offer something that is large enough that participants in the back row can see. However, because the object will be removed from view after a few minutes, it needs to be small and light enough that you can easily obscure it behind a podium (or piano or the like). Objects I have used successfully in the past: a basket, a musical instrument, a vase of flowers, a stuffed animal, even a visitor who stopped by for a moment.

Recipe (in Two Parts)

Part A

OPENING ANNOUNCEMENT

Today's theme focuses on presence and absence. Consider what presence means to you in any way. (*To leader*: I suggest writing "presence" and "absence" on the board, so that inventive minds don't creatively think you said "presents," as in gifts.)

STEPS

1. Take ten minutes to freewrite about presence and absence.
2. Discuss with a partner or as a group. (*To leader*: While they are writing, place an object on a table in front of the group.)

Part B

STEPS

1. Take a look at this object for a few minutes. You may come and observe it up close and (if appropriate) take in other properties, such as touch or smell.
2. Consider the presence of the object. Momentarily I will be removing it from view.
3. Now, from memory, return to freewriting/drawing, but this time specifically about the presence, and now absence, of this particular object. You may include the context as well, if that supports situating the object in space.

4. Start by writing a flurry of one- or two-word jottings as a word cloud, noting as many qualities of the object that you can recall. After building your word cloud, proceed to freewriting/drawing about your observation and experience.

Variation: Cloaking

Throw a blanket over the object instead of removing the item from sight. The blanket affords a different kind of "viewing": the object itself is not visible, yet the overall shape is observable.

Post-Exercise Discussion Topics

Themes that arise in group discussions include sensory memory, time, perspective, context, the relationship of presence and absence, personal associations, mysterious disappearance, traces.

Sensory Studies and Fieldwork

For a sensory fieldwork workshop I recommend emphasizing the word cloud process (Part B #4), asking the group to write as many descriptors and attributes of the absent object as they can for a solid minute. After the minute, they are asked to write a clear paragraph that offers a detailed description of the object and context. The word cloud challenge can be delivered playfully but with some urgency. I often explain that the urgency is meant to prompt a degree of gravity that mirrors being in the field and producing fieldnote jottings on the spot as reminders of a scene.

I repeat this exercise in the next workshop, but instead of a single object, I ask everyone to focus on several, in hopes that they will consider the relationships between objects, context, culture, and their perspectives.

Creativity

For many participants, "Traces, Presence" fosters their mysterious and whimsical sides. It helps to tell a story, such as the backstory that opens this exploration. I find that a story helps the group to recognize and even empathize with such an experience. By illustrating the mysterious yet puzzling encounter, they will quickly relate to how one's active mind creatively searches for a solution.

Realism is not the point. I encourage the writing, drawing, and other creative explorations to venture into the imaginary, since struggling to remember the exact appearance of the object can be frustrating. Everyone soon realizes that memory is not perfect and reveals where we are in time and perspective at any given moment. As a result, deeply insightful responses to the exploration often erupt.

Traces, Touch

Backstory and Overview

I remember attending Halloween parties where kids would be blindfolded and led through a haunted house scene. I have a feeling that many of you will recall having your hand placed in a bowl of grapes floating in oil as a spooky voice murmured something like, "Here, try some freshly harvested eyes!" While "Traces, Touch" was not modeled after these party shenanigans, the first time I tested it in a workshop, these childhood memories came rolling in.

"Traces, Touch" is a playful group activity that challenges participants' tactile sensory memory of an unknown object hidden inside of a paper bag. The point is not to spend time trying to identify what the item might be but to attempt to take in the sensory tactile information. Because it is human to want to identify and categorize, the objective of focusing on the sensory qualities is challenging. The playful unknown, especially without being able to see what one is encountering via touch, provides a wonderful playground for heightening the sensory modality of touch while encouraging creative exploration.

Unlike other sensory modalities, touch is a direct, physical sensory encounter. Tactile experiences involve numerous subcategories simultaneously, such as textural qualities or temperature. Is it smooth or scratchy? Made of glass, metal, plastic, wood? What is its temperature? Is there feedback, such as buoyancy? Are there parts of the object that can move (wheels or fur or a handle)? And so on.

Preparation (significant, for materials)

Leaders will need to prepare a number of paper bags filled with a selection of interesting objects for the workshop. Decide how many participants will work in each group; I suggest three to five per group. Divide total number of attendees by participants per group. That number equals how many objects and bags you need. I always prepare a few extra bags, just in case.

Seek objects that have a variety of tactile qualities. Items that defy identification tend to work well (although you might notice some frustrated participants!). I have collected old-fashioned clamps, truck parts, hardware, and other abstract objects. Altered or broken common objects are particularly challenging.

Recipe

OPENING ANNOUNCEMENT

Today we are playfully exploring the sense of touch and tactile memory. Please gather into groups of three to five and sit together, if possible, away from the other groups in the workshop.

STEPS

1. I will present each group with a bag that contains an object. Each person takes turns reaching into the bag to explore the item inside. Please do not look inside the bag or talk to each other. The point is not to identify what the object is, despite the human tendency to attempt to identify what one senses.
2. After everyone in your group has had ample time to explore, about ten minutes total, please write in your journal about your experience or use the experience as a sensory prompt for a narrative.
3. *To leader*: Wait until it seems everyone has finished writing and then say, "Time to take your objects out of the bags!" At this point one person from each group may hold up the object to display it for the entire group.
4. Discuss in small groups and then with the class/workshop. What did you write about? Does anyone want to share a passage?

Note to Leader

I find that some participants get overly excited, cannot remain quiet, and end up revealing what they believe the object to be. You can proactively work through this by encouraging them to keep the experience *as an exploration* and by explaining that divulging one's inner thoughts ruins the encounter for others.

Bring spare bags with objects, just in case someone does reveal the object to the others or is disappointed because they immediately identified the item and wanted more of a challenge.

Post-Exercise Discussion Topics

Participants cannot resist trying to identify the object. They often talk about imagining or "seeing" it, including colors, the materials, and other qualities they might sense.

Sensory Studies and Fieldwork

As a sensory fieldwork exercise, "Traces, Touch" offers aspects of sense that are often not included in fieldnotes. The playfulness of the exploration somehow "allows" participants to delight in the mysterious, whimsical encounter, yet they are consistently struck by the fact that touch is not a sensory modality they normally explicitly observe or notate. How might tactile qualities be incorporated in one's fieldnotes? Do tactile qualities differ from community to community? How do tactile qualities define our environment (consider the community of the blind, for example)?

Creativity

A wealth of narratives flows from the exploration! Participants never have a shortage of narratives reflecting their experience, about the fictive life of the object, or about unique tactile memories. Including drawing as well as freewriting as a possibility for an expressive response offers interesting challenges.

Traces, Surface

Backstory and Overview

When I was young my parents packed up wide rolls of rice paper, charcoal, masking tape, and bamboo brackets in a common paper shopping bag, and off we drove to old graveyards to make tombstone rubbings. While the technique of making tombstone rubbings inspired "Traces, Surface," I have altered the details of our original family outing.

Preparation (significant, for materials)

Crayons and lightweight white paper or tracing paper. The size of the paper can be standard 8½″ x 11″ sheets. You can bring in objects for participants to make rubbings, such as a textured board, coins, perforated metal plates, screens, or thickly woven fabric.

Recipe (in Two Parts)

Part A

OPENING ANNOUNCEMENT

When you were a child, did you make rubbings of pennies with crayons? Today we are going to search for interesting textures, examining only the surface elements of objects. Take a few crayons and two sheets of paper. Sharing is encouraged. One sheet is for test rubbings; the second is for your rubbing collage.

STEPS

1. Explore the surroundings. Notice surface textures of common, flat surfaces in the room (in the hallway; out on the street, if appropriate for your group). Place your paper on top of the surface and, using the side of the crayon, rub the paper so that the texture of the object below the paper surfaces.
2. Find another object and repeat.
3. Continue repeating until you have filled the paper as a collage of a wide variety of textures. The first sheet of paper may be used as a test of various surfaces and the second as the more composed or arranged collage.

Part B

STEPS

1. Using your texture collage as a prompt, take ten minutes to freewrite about the rubbing process, the outcome, or both.
2. Discuss.

Note to Leader

The workshop location is key. The point of "Traces, Surface" is the hunt for textures, so an enthusiasm for locating textures might erupt. However, if there are "precious" surfaces in the room (in a classroom, for example), be sure to request that participants remain focused and not get crayon marks on particular surfaces. I don't tend to designate areas that are "off limits," but you may want to consider your location ahead of time.

Post-Exercise Discussion Topics

Participants marvel that they never noticed surface textures and that the exploration heightened their awareness, not only during the session but for days afterward.

Many real and metaphoric themes arise from the simple exploration: texture, pattern, quality, density, surface (verb), touch, coarse and smooth, shape, and tread are just a few.

Sensory Studies and Fieldwork

An awareness of surfaces and textures can be valuable in the field. Noting how different cultures incorporate surface textures, aesthetically or for practical reasons, can be insightful (anti-slip surfaces, or surfaces created for the blind to read, for example). How do surfaces inform people and other living beings of our environment and how to navigate within those spaces?

Creativity

"Traces, Surface" can serve as an initial prompt for a variety of creativity workshops that span sculpture, drawing, collage, writing, even contact improvisation. The playful, hands-on nature of the activity provides a whimsical quality where participants explore their environment and then reflect on the process.

Reaching Out

Backstory and Overview

"Reaching Out" acknowledges local communities that are in need and identifies ways to support them as a group project. The recipe deviates from others in this book because your group will need to find a community issue close to home that speaks to your group's aims. I will provide a few examples that I hope will help spark ideas.

Sometimes interesting opportunities line up when we have our sensory and social antennae protracted. While designing a course for first-year students, I was also volunteering for a local animal shelter. The class was called Living Metaphors—Art, Text, and the Body, and I wanted to explore how people inhabit metaphors in their everyday lives through art, text, and the body. Meanwhile, at my local shelter, cats slept on newspaper-lined metal cages. The cages seemed uncomfortable. An idea hit me: why not make

FIGURE 2. "Reaching Out": a shelter kitten with her fleece "blankie."

fleece blankets for the cages with the students, who would learn to sew, embroider, and whipstitch fabric seams using yarn and heavy needles?

One of the metaphors I played with was "transition." I was reading Donald Winnicott's concept of "transitional objects" at the time, so transition metaphors flowed in my mind (Winnicott 1971; Saragnano and Seulin 2015). The parallel situations of first-year students and kittens *in transition* was not overlooked, and many interesting and emotional discussions emerged. Also, considering "transition" metaphors in our class sewing circle raised reflections on past, present, and future timescales.

To my surprise, of the twenty students in the room, few knew how to thread a needle or sew. The classroom transformed into an exciting workshop, and the group created several dozen blankets for the shelter. We called it the "Transition Blankie Project." The feel-good moments, camaraderie, and the shelter's gratitude took the humble project over the top. I'd like to add that there were several aspects to the project that contributed to a sense of well-being for the participants (students, cats, and me), including a meditative quality of mindfulness while sewing, the gifting to others (without an expectation of compensation), and gratitude. (See Manning [2004] for knitting as an approach to mindful practice.)

"Transition Blankie Project" is only one example of how connections can be made for explorations in workshops or classrooms. Other examples of

"Reaching Out" are creativity and performance workshops at elderly living centers and underprivileged day camps in the city. A few of these projects have raised enough awareness that private grants have been established to continue to support the connections.

Stirring and Plating

I encourage leaders to find ways to publicize and display your projects. In the case of the "Transition Blankie Project," the students were proud to see photographs of kittens snuggling with their blankies at the shelter. It is important that the funders (or future funders) have a selection of photographs as well.

Now!

Backstory and Overview

I bow to Pauline Oliveros for seeding this idea. She would often post on Facebook or a group e-mail a simple line, "What are you listening to?" A flurry of responses from all over the world would fly in. I wondered whether I could incorporate the idea into a multisensory conversation, and "Now!" was born. Another inspiration was learning about Mihaly Csikszentmihalyi's research method—Experience Sampling Method—where pagers were used to report on participants' everyday psychological/emotional state at the random moment they received a pager signal (Larson and Csikszentmihalyi 2014).

"Now!" urges participants to pause, sense, and respond. Rapid exchange of information in the era of e-mail and cellphone apps facilitates a type of experimental sensory prompting that can extend beyond the classroom. The basic idea of the "Now!" exercise is that the leader sends out a message to the group with a sensory prompt such as "Smell," and participants, after a sensory pause for a minute, respond with their in-the-moment experiential reflections in their current location. It is best if "Now!" is repeated several times over a few sessions, using a different sensory modality prompt. Participants become accustomed to the rapid-fire prompt-respond loop. During the following meeting the leader facilitates a discussion for participants to share their individual sensory experiences and how the "Now!" practice revealed issues about sensory awareness.

Sample anonymous responses can be found in the "Resources" chapter at the close of the book.

Preparation (little to none)

During a group meeting the leader describes the recipe for "Now!" It is vital that participants are aware they will receive a mysterious e-mail prompt at a random moment in their week and understand that a quick response is appreciated. I tend to include in the first e-mail a review of the "Now!" exercise; see below for examples. Leaders will need to collect participants' responses and include them in a single document for the next group meeting.

Recipe

OPENING ANNOUNCEMENT

During the week, at an undisclosed time, I will send out an e-mail or text to the group with the subject line "Now!"

STEPS

1. Upon receiving the message, take thirty to sixty seconds to sit with eyes closed and focus on the sensory modality specified in the e-mail. For example, if the sensory modality is vision, sit for a few seconds with eyes closed, then open them and note your visual surroundings.
2. Take a few additional minutes to convey your experience—through a written, drawn, photographed, or other medium—and e-mail it to me. (Depending on your group, a blog may work.)
3. The individual "Now!" responses will be shared (unless specified not to) at the next gathering of the group for a discussion.

Note to Leader

Consider the process for sharing the responses. In my workshops with twenty or fewer participants, I collect the responses but do not tag them with participants' names. I either project the responses in the room or print and distribute them. Alternately, I print only one copy and ask participants to read them out loud (not necessarily their own).

Example Prompt

The following is an actual e-mail that I sent to participants. Feel free to use the language or create your own. More example texts are listed below.

This week's challenge

Here is the sensory challenge for this week. It is a bit unusual, but bear with me:

- Three times during the week I will e-mail you with the subject line "Now!"
- When you receive this e-mail please close your eyes, pause for a minute and . . . listen! What do you hear? Be open to the field of sound you are inhabiting both inside and outside of the body.
- **Respond to my e-mail** with a handful of words, sentences that reflect what you experienced during this minute. Please do not overthink. Sense, then respond.
- The aim is to respond promptly to elicit a flow between experience and expression of what is sensed. Engage with the "Now!" exploration as soon as you receive the message and can respond.

Stirring and Plating

The discussion can be the most stimulating part of the exercise. I make a particular point to the group that the "Now!" reflections are not meant to be critiqued but instead viewed as a multilocation array of sensibilities experienced by the class. I strongly believe that sensory ownership of one's experience is vital, and the knowledge that participants will not be judged by their expressive outpourings deeply encourages quick, raw, creative responses. Their requirement is to purely be present by pausing and sensing.

The sensory modalities change from week to week, depending on the workshop or class intensity. The prompts aim to encourage participants to continuously expand awareness of their physical and psychological relationship to their present environment. If the heightened awareness occurs only during the workshop or class, the effect is not as strong. Encouraging participants to engage while away from the group can act as a segue to heightening awareness in everyday life.

Effusive responses arise the next time participants gather in person after a "Now!" prompt. Those who normally don't speak happily share their experience. In fact, they honestly own their experiences freely. "Now!" fosters group discussion, and even if included only a few times over the course of a session/semester, the recipe serves this particular purpose.

How Often?

The frequency of "Now!" prompts depends on the specific class or workshop I am teaching. For example, participants can receive between one and three prompts per week when I teach classes on creativity, the senses, or sensory ethnography.

I have noticed that there can be confusion or even a bit of resistance during the first week. All I need to say to both students (and to you as leaders) is—carry on! During the next class discussion, clarify the challenge and repeat the exercise. In the case of "Now!," I find that persistent practice and discussion about the process benefits everyone.

Participants may need time to realize that there is no "right" or "wrong." I remind them that there are no specific expectations *except e-mail responses* to the prompt. Despite initial resistance or confusion, I notice that participants eventually experience a liberating feeling simply because they recognize that the exercise is for their benefit, not merely an assignment to generate a grade. The liberating sensibility can be quite dramatic. Periodically students e-mail me months after the semester reporting a sensory realization, liberating affect, practice-based understanding, or other shift of awareness.

Now! Examples

Below I offer several e-mail examples that I have developed over the years. You'll notice that I've altered the prompt depending upon the sensory modality. Most often, the simpler, the better. I encourage you to e-mail your group using your own voice. However, if my prompts work for you, please use them!

Subject heading: Now! smell

The key is to respond as soon as possible (in other words, try NOT to think about it, just respond to the prompt). Whenever you receive this, take thirty seconds to tune in to your environment with a heightened awareness.

- Close your eyes and breathe, focusing on what you smell.
- What do you smell right NOW?
- Respond . . .
- E-mail me a few lines.

Your response doesn't need to be in perfectly written sentences. Just respond intuitively. Your reflection on smell need not be extreme. *Note what you are able to sense.*

If you are not in a location that affords any kind of reflection on smell, go ahead and take a moment to move location.

Subject heading: Now! touch

When you receive this e-mail, please *continue* your activities for the next twenty minutes or so and be aware of your tactile sense . . .

- What do you feel?
- Feel free to include your tactile sense of inner and/or outer body.
- Respond to my e-mail with a handful of words and/or sentences and/or a photo that reflects what you experienced during this minute. (If it is a photo, limit the size.)

Subject heading: Now! taste

Next time you are eating, drinking, or tasting something, dwell with the sensation for thirty to sixty seconds and send me your reflection (words, drawings, photos, etc.). Should you want to send a photo, please do add some text as well.

Subject heading: Now! listen

When you receive this, take thirty seconds to tune in to your environment with a heightened awareness to sound.

Listening . . .

- What sounds are you aware of?
- Respond: E-mail me a few lines. Your response doesn't need to be in perfectly written sentences. Just respond intuitively.

Sensory Studies and Fieldwork

I have found that checking in with a group via e-mail works for some groups more than others. It depends on the individuals in the group and their relationship to e-mail. "Now!" is a good fit for groups working to develop their sensory fieldwork practice and vocabulary. Because the exploration may be prompted at any random time during the week, participants often reflect that it keeps their everyday awareness of various sensations sharp and not just "turned on" when conducting fieldwork. The exploration also reminds participants that multisensory awareness is vital and that the community they are studying may have a very different sensory orientation.

Creativity

"Now!" not only provides impromptu on-the-spot creativity but also promotes a sense of well-being by resetting one's focus for one or two minutes. Participants remark that it encourages a mini-meditation of sorts, where introspection fuels a creative response, and notice how their accumulated raw responses, just as they are, embody poetic qualities. We discuss spacing and form of text on the page.

Banding

Backstory and Overview

"The question, Me? You? Us? becomes at once appropriate but totally unanswerable. As I cannot feel any differentiation—I am me.you.us. I feel it. Your pulse rocks the band that nudges my ankle that glides across the floor that takes your belly with it. And down to the ground you go. And then I. And you. And I. And you. us. I. continually. It is at the point where: We have become the same project" (Lindsay Vogt in Hahn et al. 2016, 153).

"The inadequacy of words emphasizes the body expressing. Perhaps this is why I have become drawn to making music with an instrument that has such an uncompromised relationship with the body—the sound only exists in relation to the body's essential process of breathing and the contours of

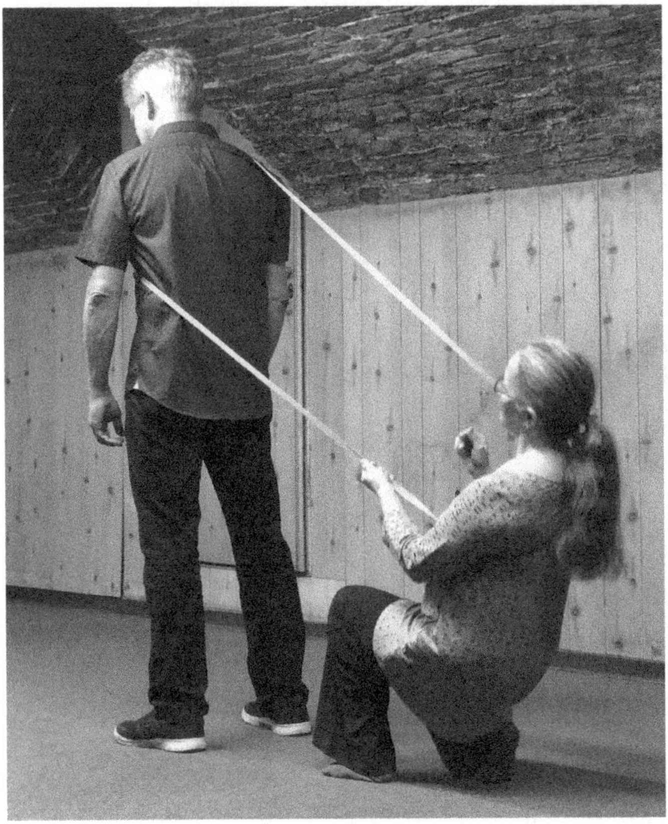

FIGURE 3. Banding demonstration, Pavia, Italy, 2018.

the sound directly reflect the internal contours of the body" (Simon Rose in Hahn et al. 2016, 154).

The two passages above are excerpts from two musicians' journals reflecting their experiences during experimental movement and sound improvisation sessions called "banding," where participants are literally connected by giant rubber bands as they improvise. Lindsay's and Simon's texts grapple with how to articulate the essence of new multisensory experiences and creative expressions with others through a shared object.

"Banding" is an experimental exercise in movement and sound improvisation I have been developing since 2008. During banding sessions, participants can "feel" the movement and presence of those they are banded with. I cannot stress strongly enough how profound the responses have been. Banding has become a contemplative practice that I incorporate into diversity and communication sessions for a wide variety of participants ranging in age from ten to eighty years old. Banding has also fostered collaborations with psychologists, cognitive scientists, and neuroscientists to explore a range of topics. (See Hahn and Jordan 2017 and Hahn et al. 2016 for examples.)

FIGURE 4. Group banding, Marlboro, Vermont, 2011.

Preparation (significant)

This recipe works best with a group of at least ten participants. You will need ten or more large rubber pallet bands; those measuring between seventy-two and ninety-two inches work well. (Suppliers of pallet bands include ULINE and Global Industrial.) An open space is also necessary.

Demonstration

I always include a demonstration of banding with a volunteer so that all participants visually see the strength of the bands. Pallet bands are designed to hold large boxes together on pallets, generally for shipping transport on trucks or airplanes. That means that the bands are engineered to be incredibly strong.

Recipe

Round 1: Sensitizing Level

STEPS

1. Place large pallet bands in the middle of the floor. Working in pairs, place a band around an arm, elbow, torso, or wrist and attach it to your partner's arm, elbow, torso, or wrist.
2. Start by turning away from each other and exploring various levels of pull via the band. Begin very slowly, with little tension in the band. Can you sense your partner's subtle movements? What are the qualities of movement that you can sense? Changes in body positions, such as an angling upward, or to one side? Speed of movement? Can you also sense other qualities, such as fatigue? reluctance? enthusiasm? Does closing your eyes change the experience? Explore the slow dynamic of improvisation as you gain trust and awareness.
3. After a period of improvisation (ten to twenty minutes, depending on the group), remove the bands and transition from banding to writing without conversation. Freewrite about anything that comes to mind. Include drawings or other forms of creative expression reflections in your notebook.

Round 2: Safe Play, Eyes Open!

In Round 1 we began in pairs. After their freewriting I will ask the participants to band again for Round 2. At this time I hand additional bands to these groups and ask that they "attach" to other groups, forming larger groups. Eventually, the entire group will be interconnected.

STEPS

1. Working in groups of three to five people, attach bands to legs, arms, torso, hips.
2. Now facing in any direction, *eyes open*, explore the dynamics of a group in flow—with no limitations of speed, direction, or where the bands are attached. What are the mechanics of pull when there are several people in a group connected by bands? What is the difference between Round 1 and Round 2?

Round 3: Sound Banding

STEPS

1. Continuing from Round 2 groups or beginning a new round, everyone now add sound to their movement explorations. Does the addition of sound change the experience? Does the movement improvisation change with sound?
2. Freewrite and/or freedraw about the experience.

Note to Leader

Although I listed ten or more participants, it is possible to band with as few as six. The largest group I have banded together included well over one hundred participants.

Post-Exercise Discussion Topics

Feeling of (inter)connectedness with others. Also, the feeling of being connected even after the bands have been removed. Empathy for others.

Trust and awareness of other participants' sensitivities.

Topics related to tactile sensory awareness, sound and vibration, movement and kinesthesia, emotion, and the senses.

Sensations of presence of others through movement and pull through the bands.

Relationships between people.

Sensory Studies and Fieldwork

Awareness of tactile and kinesthetic sensory modalities are not as common in sensory studies and fieldwork projects. I believe the insights gained in practicing and developing one's awareness of touch and movement can provide a depth of understanding about other people, including relationships, spatial orientation, the sense of presence, and sensitivities to connectedness. Banding conjures a deep, tangible awareness of trust, and the playful activity can raise these issues in a safe setting prior to embarking on fieldwork, where the metaphoric and very real concerns about well-being and trust might arise.

Creativity

Banding can be included as a contemplative practice, a creative movement and sound exploration, and creative practice to enable (embodied and verbal) communication in diverse communities. Because of the deeply visceral sensory immersion during banding, the reality of embodied learning, communication, and embodied knowledge is immediately understood. One of my collaborators, cognitive psychologist Scott Jordan, noted that the visual quality of seeing the bands connecting individuals makes visible what is normally invisible in communication. One theater group I collaborated with was just at the point of learning their lines in a Shakespeare play. We banded together characters who had dialogue or emotional "ties" and watched as the reality of their connections and struggles became visible. Once the bands were removed, the actors found that the sense of connectedness remained. Similarly, improvisers, including musicians and dancers, will often say that they feel connections during improvisation and that the bands make visible what was present but not visible.

Rolling Time

Overview

Can one's sense of time be a sensory modality? Is anticipation a sensory modality? Is kinesthesia? "Rolling Time" aims to reveal participants' sense of time via their experiential awareness of anticipation and movement. Participants are led through simple stages to unravel how multiple sensations simultaneously inform their anticipatory, embodied knowledge. As with many of the experimental exercises in this collection, "Rolling Time" challenges participants to dive deeper into their sensory awareness. Particularly important will be noting *embodied* forward-looking, anticipatory sensibilities alongside the physics of inertia. How are anticipation and inertia embodied? What influences our sense of time? Can we even "see through" our own cultural constructions of our sense of time *while* existing in time?

As usual, the exercise is deliberately simple but hopefully will reveal deeper, introspective insights. There are five stages of "Rolling Time." Leaders may select any number of the stages that seem appropriate for their group's needs. Consider these stages as variants on the theme of anticipation:

A. Memory Rolling
B. Rolling in the Real World
C. Hold It!
D. Comparisons
E. Group Improvisation

Preparation (minimal)

Things you will need: a variety of objects *that have the potential* to roll but roll differently, such as a pencil, ball, bell, apple, cup.

Recipe (in Five Parts)

Part A: Memory Rolling

OPENING ANNOUNCEMENT

Please have your notebooks and pens ready. Today we will consider our sense of movement and anticipation.

STEPS

1. Sit in a comfortable position. Close your eyes. From your memory, recall a specific, familiar object rolling.
2. Consider the context, the environment. We'll sit in silence for about three minutes to contemplate. Be as specific as possible about the features of the object, the environment it is in, and the surface it is rolling on. How specific can you be?
3. Consider all of the sensory qualities and context that affect the rolling affair—sonic, kinesthetic, tactile, visual. What is the weather like? Is the ground smooth or rough or slanted? And so on.
4. After one to three minutes of focused contemplation, open your eyes. Please jot down and/or draw in your journal your observations.
5. Discuss. *To leader*: I often ask someone to lead our discussion each session, to call on participants and move the discussion along. I tell them that "leading" in our case means allowing others to speak without too much guidance or prompting at first. Opening a group talk can be as

simple as "Any thoughts?" or "What thoughts arose?" Once everyone has spoken or the discussion comes to a natural close, adding a few questions or prompts can help move the discussion ahead.

Questions for follow-up can include these:

- Did you imagine watching or hearing the object roll?
- Was it difficult for you to visualize the rolling scene?
- What was the nature of the roll?
- If you imagined movement, did it convey information about enactive knowledge and the object, even though the scene was one that was imagined?
- Did the rolling make sound?
- Did the surface texture of the object affect the roll?
- What color and shape was the object?

Part B: Rolling in the Real World

To leader: Find an actual object to roll. The object does not need to be a ball. In fact, I find it interesting to compare rolling a smooth ball with another unlikely roller, such as a lightbulb, a pencil, a walnut, or a wad of crunched-up paper. Each possesses unique qualities to observe.

STEPS

1. Please bring out your notebooks. Observe the nature of this object rolling, including my initiation of the movement.
2. *To leader*: Roll the object for the group. The roll can be repeated, especially for comparison.
3. Everyone observe the attributes of the roll, including as much detail as possible, and log them in your journal. For those working without a group: if there is someone nearby, ask that person to roll the object, preferably on the floor. If you prefer to work solo or if no one is around, put the object on the floor and mobilize the roll with your foot.
4. Discuss. Was the object rolled slowly? Was it kicked, tapped, tossed? Was the object rolled with a flick of a wrist? What was your collaborator's posture? Motion coordination? How might anticipation have influenced your experience?

Part C: Hold It!

OPENING ANNOUNCEMENT

Time to hold the object to gather further information. How might tactile information lead us to new or different knowledge?

STEPS

1. Pass around the object. (Sometimes I bring in several of the same object to make it easier.)
2. Allow the object to rock in your palm. (Should the object be a bowling ball, this might be a challenge!) Be creative and adapt at will. The purpose in Part C is to directly engage with the object: touch it and feel its weight, density, smoothness, roughness, irregularities, and quality of movement in your palm.
3. Record as many observations as you can in your notebook.

Part D: Comparisons

STEPS

1. Consider these issues: What memories or observations surfaced in Parts A and B that were similar, or different? Do you believe that Part A might have influenced your observations in Part B?

   What sensory attributes constitute "rolling"? How do the characteristics of the object, the surface it rolls on, the person rolling the object, or the environment (wind, floor evenness or level, other objects in the room, or people, for example) contribute to the roll? How about your own mood or present focus during the activity?
2. Note as many observations as you can in your notebook.

Part E: Group Improvisation

If your group gathers to focus on performance (music, theater, or movement, for example), I strongly suggest that members take "Rolling Time" to another level. After completing one or more of the recipe stages, try regrouping to rehearse the piece members are currently working on. It can be any ensemble piece, whether improvised or composed. Directly shift to a playing session. Ask that the participants not engage in discussion prior to playing. Afterward, ask the group if they found that the exploration influenced the session in any way.

Post-Exercise Discussion Topics

Hopefully the issues raised in the introduction of "Rolling Time" naturally surface during the group discussion. Awareness of anticipation related to movement, sound, and time often emerge.

If participants raise a specific case from their experience that seems to lean toward a larger issue, the leader might request deeper unpacking of their rolling encounter. Although it normally takes more time to unpack experiences through group discussion, in my opinion it is best when the participants arrive at larger concepts on their own and/or through discussion, given enough time in the session.

The particulars of personal experience often reveal general issues that can be discussed by the group.

Sensory Studies and Fieldwork

For groups exploring sensory awareness, the theme of anticipation can raise many insights and questions. How might sensory studies illuminate and also document anticipation? While "Rolling Time" focused on movement, sound, and touch, how might anticipation of any sensory quality provide insights into time? Might anticipation be another sense? Are personal experiences of anticipation entrained physical coordinations that are enculturated into our consciousness? What about psychological awareness and assumptions?

Creativity

I have found that the whimsical nature of "Rolling Time" encourages participants to interact in playful ways. In several workshops I was delighted to see participants create their own variants of the exploration. No doubt, the presence of several kinds of balls in the room inspired play! I encourage drawing in their journal entries to creatively convey movement, time, and anticipation. I have noticed dramatic pen strokes, arrows, and textures in their journals, and these jottings often become drafts for new artistic design projects.

Circles, a Sound and Movement Exploration

Overview

I thoroughly enjoyed sitting in on Pauline Oliveros's Deep Listening classes and workshops. They gave me an opportunity to watch the uplifting and playful qualities of her delivery of many of her "Sonic Meditations" (Oliveros 1974). While I was designing "Circles," Pauline welcomed me to workshop it in her class and gave me feedback. Thank you, Pauline!

The aim of "Circles" is for participants to gain a heightened awareness of sound and movement. Participants stand in a circle and "gift" a sound as fluidly as possible around the circle. The group attempts to keep the continuity, or flow, of the sound as it travels around the circle.

Specific aims include

- listening intently;
- focusing on the task of transforming a sound that is provided in-the-moment (this is not just a repetition of, or *re*acting to, the sound given but transforming it);
- noticing changes in quality, pitch, duration, and intensity;
- considering shape and flow of sound (not only melodies but how the four parameters of sound contribute to the shape and flow of sound);
- responding and observing, while not being disruptive to the community;
- noting continuity of sound within the circle;
- being aware of one's own sounds/movements, of individuals within the group, and of the group as a whole;
- being aware of the relationships of movements and sounds; and
- expanding one's sound/movement vocabulary through collaboration and improvisation.

Preparation (little to none)

Leaders, consider what vocal sound you will begin with, preferably one that strongly implies direction, flow, and continuity. For example, try starting with a high pitch that glides downward rapidly.

Recipe (in Two Parts)

Part A

STEPS

1. Everyone stand up and form a large circle so that you can see each person in the group (four to six inches apart, depending on how many are in the group).
2. Let's begin our circle of sound. I will start by "gifting" the person to my right a vocal sound. Please vocalize only a NON-referential *vocal* sound and "pass it" along to the next person.

   (*Note to leader*: proactively provide examples of what "referential sound" means, such as "bowwow," "cock-a-doodle-doo," "ticktock," etc.)
3. On the fly, note the shape of the sound that the person gifts to you. Also note the quality (timbre), duration, and intensity.
4. Your job is to **pick up** the sound at the tail end of my vocalizing, **transform it,** and pass a new sound to the next person, and so on. Overlap-

ping the sounds helps continuity. Please minimize talking, giggling or distracting others so we can complete our circle!

(*Note to leader*: The first time I start with a rather dramatic and distinct vocalization.)

5. *Remember* what sound you made, because we will continue around the circle several times and you will need to repeat your sound as closely as possible on the next few rounds. See if we can make the sounds flow around the circle *as if it was one long phrase*, smooth and fluid.

   (*Note to leader*: It can take a couple of tries to get completely around the circle even one time.)
6. Continue to pass the sound around the circle at least three times.

   (*Note to leader*: During the second pass you could call out "Faster!" and later "As slow as possible!")
7. Stop to celebrate and discuss.

   (*Note to leader*: I generally create closure by uttering my final vocalization and then turn to the group to ask: Anyone have observations?)

We often run "Circles" a few more times, with new sounds, before moving on to Part B.

Part B

In the discussion above, usually someone notices that *gaze and body movements assisted the timing and passing along of sound*. If so, great! Their awareness of movement and sound improvisation is surfacing. Now that the awareness of the pragmatic aspects of movement is in the air, start a new iteration and purposely add movement expressivity.

OPENING ANNOUNCEMENT

Congratulations, you worked together to smoothly create one phrase. Now, let's challenge ourselves to add a movement to your vocalizing.

Let's begin a new circle. This time I'll "gift" a sound *and* movement to the next person.

To leader: A few tips:

- Use your upbeat, energetic personae to "drive" the circle forward, cheering them on, changing the pace midstream.
- Rule out (in the beginning) nonvocal sounds (stomping or clapping).
- Rule out referential sounds: any words or sounds such as "ouch," "achoo," or "bowwow" (because creativity is stifled with preformed sounds that also have meaning).

- Acknowledge that giggles will arise! Giggles pop up from the sheer silliness but often out of discomfort. I note that it happens but request that everyone try very hard not to giggle.
- Reinforce that everyone needs to remember the sound they made because when their turn comes again, they will repeat their vocalization (while still connecting it to others' sounds).
- Encourage the *transformation*, not just a repetition of what the person before vocalized.

Variation 1: Words

Try the exercise with words only, where each participant introduces a new word to form a narrative. Follow with a discussion to talk about topics such as meaning, narrative, symbolic knowledge, and expressivity.

Variation 2: Difficult!

If you have a large group (twenty or more), divide the participants into separate circles. Ask them to initiate the same recipe but urge everyone to listen to the entire room, including phasing of the circles' sounds, or noting what sounds punctuated the phrases, and so on. In a way, I am asking them to be participants in their own group while also "flies on the wall," listening to the other groups and the sound of the entire room. For many, this is a very challenging exercise, even if the participants are musicians who perform in large ensembles. Follow with a discussion.

Sensory Studies and Fieldwork

"Circles" works well for encouraging complex multisensory awareness. For example, ask participants to observe and recall sounds coordinated with movements, eye contact, facial expression, and presence.

I have incorporated the exploration in workshops for sensory fieldwork, although I reserve it for a session after the first month of classes, as it works best when participants know each other and feel less self-conscious. The exploration is quite playful and can liven up a low energy period of a semester during a university course. Shy students, in particular, might feel inhibited and out of place. I'm genuinely pleased when introvert personality types suddenly come out of their shell during the exploration.

Creativity

I always include "Circles" in workshops and classes integrating creativity. "Circles" works well with children and mixed-age groups. For gatherings of performers, who are accustomed to experimenting and being in the spotlight, I include this exploration as a kind of icebreaker to facilitate interpersonal communication. I have also used "Circles" at ethnomusicology conferences to warm up the room for "speed mentoring" sessions. One year there were over a hundred participants in the room, and they noted how it focused the large group and also created an uplifting atmosphere.

Inner Voice-Overs

Backstory and Overview

Years ago, while considering how to notate movement for research and my creative practice, I experimented with recording my process of talking through movements. Listening back, I understood these audio documents both as a process for recall of embodied knowledge and as "pieces" themselves. Later, I noted that those pesky inner voices that most notably reveal themselves during meditation provide a window into the state of body and mind. Why not appropriate and make some inner thoughts public, to acknowledge them and also learn from them? The convergence of these two experiences inspired the "Inner Voice-Overs" exploration.

"Inner Voice-Overs" draws attention to movements of the body through conscious declaration of body-mind movement processing. The exercise helps participants maintain awareness of their embodied subconscious as well as their priorities and what sensibilities become muted because of their focused attention elsewhere.

Groups tend to be very different in energy, enthusiasm, and willingness to experiment and step beyond their comfort zone. I tend to offer the exploration once I have a clear idea of the various individuals in the group. During a semester I generally observe the group for at least two to three weeks before introducing this recipe.

This recipe also works well for those working alone.

Preparation (little to none)

A room that is open affords larger movement and group work, but it is not essential.

Recipe (for Working Solo or in a Group)

STEPS

1. Start in a comfortable position, either standing, sitting, or reclining.
2. Move one hand while narrating its movement to a new position. The narration can be "spoken" inside your head or out loud, depending on how you feel at the moment. Try both and note the difference! Try it with eyes closed, then eyes open. Another option is to create an audio recording of your experiment to glean for insights later.
3. Expanded version: moving several parts of the body, what is revealed in your "inner voice-overs"?

Note to Leader

Here is an example voice-over from my archives. In this exercise, I was sitting on the floor and gently covering my left eye with my left hand.

> The left side of my face feels warm. Darkness. Pressure along my eye socket.
>
> I feel the effort of my entire arm, up the shoulder and to my neck in order to cup my eye.
>
> Moving my palm away from my eye, the fingers depart from my face at slightly different times. I hear subtle sounds of fingers brushing my eyebrows. Wrist adjusts slightly to engage the movement. Left side of face cools. Elbow draws downward, as my lower arm and hand move forward, unhinging only at the elbow. Left hand rotates to palm down. I am pressing my left palm to my knee, exerting pressure. I lean back in my chair and tilt my head back.

This brief example spotlights how the exploration draws attention to a single limb's movement through narration. However, despite the fact that I singled out one limb, the narration quickly reveals that a variety of sensibilities and parts of the body come into play. *Note what is not included in the narration.* In many ways what is not included reveals my sensory focus, what I am conscious of, what I prioritized, and the details I was able to attend to at the moment. I can then curiously ask myself why I prioritized or "randomly" selected a particular path.

The solo version affords privacy. Here, one can talk out loud and not feel self-conscious, if that is a temperament at play. If you create an audio or video recording of the exercise, try transcribing your utterings. Note what you experience while transcribing. I often experience a physical reliving of the moment while transcribing movement and sound, which I imagine stands as a testimony to embodied knowledge and memory.

Group Activity Overview

Although based on the same basic exercise, in many ways the group version stands as an entirely different activity. The leader needs to be attuned to the degree to which the participants may feel comfortable or not. Some might be self-conscious moving and/or speaking out loud, while others are excited to experiment. Again, I tend to run "Inner Voice-Overs" once I know the individuals in the group.

In most groups I run the exercise with silent inner voice-overs first. After observing their progress and listening to the group discussion, I gauge whether to step up the challenge that day or reserve it for the next session.

Variation 1

Describe the activity to the group as in the recipe above. The first round will use voice-overs that are inside the conscious mind. At the close of the one-minute movement exercise, the movers write down what has transpired to the best of their memory.

Variation 2

Repeat the recipe but have only half of the group move and the other half observe. *Note*: Let the group members know that they will be switching roles. The movement should be simple *and repeatable*. Often it is easier for the movers to do a pantomime of a common activity (one participant in my group, for example, worked at a pizza shop and had quite an elaborate minute of movement drawn from memory).

Observers watch and take in as much information as they can about the mover's phrase. After the one-minute movement presentation, both movers and observers take quick notes in their notebooks about the movement phrase, then they switch roles. Discussion follows.

Variation 3

This can be considered a performance piece . . . a happening! I find participants, even the shy ones, really appreciate this "wild version" of "Inner Voice-Overs."

The group leader needs to let the group know ahead of time approximately how long the happening will be. I often say something like, "In five minutes I will ring a bell to signal a thirty-second wrap-up."

Everyone, including the leader if possible, stands and moves in the room. A lot of movement is not necessary. Participants speak out loud their voice-overs in strong, audible voices. (*Note to leader*: one session I asked everyone to whisper and the result was dramatic.) The group leader signals the wrap-up, and then miraculously the piece begins to wind down. Ask participants to take a moment to write a few words of reflection (to help prompt discussion).

Sensory Studies and Fieldwork

Participants in sensory studies workshops have effusively commented on the liberating nature of the exploration. In discussions, realizations arose that participants normally try pushing away their inner thoughts and views. Participants marveled that the encouragement and "permission" to let inner comments be voiced exposed thoughts as reports of where the mind was directed from moment to moment. Some participants found that the exploration raised their empathetic awareness of others' movements, sounds, and thoughts.

Creativity

The playful nature of "Inner Voice-Overs" animates a room while also allowing for deeper, introspective insights. Groups working on creative experimentation easily take on the "wild version." Variants that arose spontaneously from group members have included splitting the group in half so that some of the participants free-improvised to create a soundscape to blend in with the voices. Participants' practice of reinventing the explorations encouraged everyone's experimentation.

Body Parts

Backstory and Overview

As a child I verbally created sound effects while playing. As a colossal robot, the sounds of my footsteps on the earth made terrifying rumbling sounds; as a cowboy, my lasso whipped and whistled in the air; when my toy cars, airborne, crashed into the sandbox . . . *Kri-i-i- ashhhh!!* Admit it. You probably did this too. Fast forward a few decades . . .

While collaborating with composer and interface designer Curtis Bahn to develop the interactive sonic character Pikapika, we spontaneously discovered a creative practice for "auditioning" sounds for the character based on my body movement–sound coordination. Then, for a residency for interface design we noticed the programmer-designers creating interfaces for performance were not necessarily "in" their bodies—meaning, they would design an interface without using their own physical, kinesthetic, sensory knowledge. Instead, they would create an interface and hand it to the performer, who would try to use it and provide comments to the designer. The design process remained a cyclic feedback system. However, when the designers, programmers, dancers, and musicians were all asked to improvise together in the "Body Parts" exploration, interesting "eureka" moments arose (see Hahn and Bahn [2002] for an account of our process and Hahn and Bahn [2004] for footage of the piece; see Hahn [2015] for a published version of this exercise in poetic form).

"Body Parts" helps participants visualize, localize, and then embody sound in a playful yet direct way. Leaders ask participants to select a body part such as a limb and to sonify an imagined "voice" of that limb. An improvisation ensues, followed by a discussion. "Inner Voice-Overs" and "Body Parts" work well together as there are similarities, yet different creative, contemplative, and intellectual issues are raised.

Preparation (little to none)

It is helpful to bring a bell to the session to help provide the closure without too much disruption.

If the room has a floor that is clean, start with everyone lying down, knees up, feet flat, eyes closed.

If the floor is filthy, start with everyone standing, feet hip-width apart, eyes closed. If you know ahead of time about the floor's condition, ask participants to bring in yoga mats or large towels.

Recipe (in Two Parts)

Part A: Settling In

STEPS

1. Everyone find a comfortable position. Settle in. Breathe in deeply. Breathe out. Notice the belly rising and falling. As you exhale, allow

your body to rest and settle. Let's repeat this as a group twice more. Breathe in . . . breathe out.

2. Draw your attention to a specific body part. This first round, selecting a limb or your head might be easiest. (*To leader*: Take your time. Allow them to settle into this stage.)
3. Visualize the body part. Consider the details in your imagination. (*To leader*: Again, give them more time than you expect. If you feel ready to move on to #4, push yourself to extend the time for this stage.)
4. Draw your attention to your navel or a central area of your body and SLOWLY visualize the energy line between that central space, all the way to your selected body part, and then flowing outward, beyond the body. In other words, imagine the energy flowing to the body part and then beyond the body.

   (Example: body part selected = tip of fingers on the right hand. Visualize the energy pathway from the belly, up the torso, ribs, chest, armpit, shoulder, upper arm, elbow, lower arm, wrist, and hand and flowing out the fingertips.)
5. Allow yourself to relax but also be aware of your flow of energy. Breathe.
6. Discuss.

Part B: Sounding!

STEPS

1. Maintaining your focus on energy flow, everyone come to a standing position. Keep your eyes closed or gaze at the floor with the eyelids half closed.
2. Imagine that the body part you selected can generate a sound when it animates. What would that sound be? When the body part moves, ***vocalize*** the sound.
3. Move the rest of the body and note how your movement changes the sound.
4. Gradually open your eyes. Note others in the room and their movements and sounds. Can you interact and find ways to change their movement and sound worlds? (*To leader*: Ring the bell to signal closure.)
5. Please do not talk. Go directly to your notebooks and freewrite/freedraw for five minutes.
6. Discuss.

Variation

If there is time, I ask two or three people to form a duet/trio and repeat the exercise while others observe. Ask the observers to have blank paper to write/draw their observations.

Sensory Studies and Fieldwork

"Body Parts" raises attention to energy flow. Various cultures' beliefs around energy flow in and outside the body reveal themselves quickly during discussions. My Japanese traditional dance and Reiki training provides me with a foundation for demonstrating ki-energy flow (and prana in my yoga training) in subsequent workshops, but such a background would not be essential for offering this recipe. A discussion between Parts A and B is vital to enable in-depth conversations about the senses and culture. If the topic does not naturally arise, I ask the group, "What does 'energy flow' mean to you? Did you feel it during the exploration?"

Creativity

"Body Parts" provides an approachable means to explore improvisation. I have noticed that both performers and nonperformers quickly catch on because they are simply enacting what I am requesting. Once they take in the entire room, moving and making sounds, it's too late to be inhibited because they are already performing. Similar to sensory fieldwork workshops, the discussions are eye-openers.

Forming Time

Overview

Here's a recipe for a simple group collaboration challenge that urges participants to consider form while creating time-based mediums. I say "simple"; however, for many participants it will be a wild ride. Generally, I offer "Forming Time" once the group has discussed the basic concepts of structure, composition, and form and they have listened to and watched performances of music and movement.

Preparation (little to none)

Prior to class or workshop, the leader has several options. Does "performance" include only movement? Or sound? Or does anything go?

I find that offering "Forming Time" several times over the course of a semester, or as several day workshops, helps. For example, I might offer the collaboration as a sound performance (only) first, then as a movement performance, and then as "anything goes."

To add drama to the challenge, say nothing. Instead, just write on the board "There will be a performance at 11 A.M. Form a group of three to five participants. Use anything *except musical instruments* to create a five-minute piece. See you at 11:00."

Recipe

STEPS

1. Gather in small groups of three to five people. Create a name for your group.
   (Option: leader creates small groups, especially if self-organized groups tend to comprise the same individuals each time.)
2. (*Leader*) Announcement: There will be a five-minute performance by each group starting at *11 A.M.* Use anything in the room *excluding* musical instruments to create sound for your performance.
3. Performance!
   To leader: Audience members need to be attentive. I ask that they write the name of the group that is performing and their own name at the top of a blank sheet of paper. They then write down their observations of the performance. Emphasize that observations need to address details of form and not merely "I liked it" or "Suzie did a great job; she's my best friend." The observations are submitted, but it's important to state that they do not impact grades (if grades are part of the scene).
4. Discuss.

Sensory Studies and Fieldwork

In a sensory studies context, "Forming Time" helps move along the discussion of what might be considered "performance" for different communities, including sensory attributes. Time-based activities such as sports, music, dance, ritual, theater, and games, as well as everyday tasks, can be challenging to analyze, and "Forming Time" can directly address the perception of time and form. The practice of building a time-based piece from the bottom up contrasts with the top-down nature of ethnography, yet the opportunity to fully experience time in collaboration with others can provide many insights. Often the topic of rituals and performance arise.

Creativity

The time pressure of creating a five-minute piece in a short period resembles a game, and workshop participants rise to the challenge by immediately racing around the room to see what objects in the room or in their knapsacks can make sound. "Forming Time" remains a favorite challenge in my workshops, and the discussions include how they needed to creatively think outside the box to locate sound objects and then create their soundscape.

Through the Portal

Backstory and Overview

Waking up from a vivid, sensory-rich dream, I found the wrenching transition to everyday life a strain. After the experience I began to write a few short stories that were structured around a transition, a portal of some kind. The compositional device challenged my contemplation of the senses, existence, and how my sensory-rich storytelling could orient me in everyday life. Sentience. The potential of shifting between "realms" is a trope used throughout history, from Zhuangzi (or Chuang-tzu) to Kafka to contemporary sci-fi plots. Nevertheless, knowledge about other realms does not make the dream-to-reality experience effortless.

"Through the Portal" challenges participants to consider the organization of time and form through sensory transitions. Specifically, the group takes on several writing sessions to construct a narrative that contains a portal. The challenge is for the character(s) in the narrative to go through a portal (literal or imagined) that shifts the story in time or location or in any way the authors please. The group initially has twenty minutes to map out their first story. The idea of transitions as part of a compositional device can be employed in a number of ways.

The next dimension of the challenge (see the variation below) resides in the ability to notice and create literal transitions (as compositional devices) to more abstract "portals," such as a musical or movement/dance transition.

Preparation (moderate)

You will find two very different "Through the Portal" example stories written by my students in the "Resources" chapter at the close of the book: Michael Schrider's "17 Years as a Beat Cop" and Amelia Farquharson's "Beyond Realism." Make enough copies for everyone in the group, but do not hand them out at the beginning of the workshop.

Note: Schrider's piece is short and works well in a workshop. However, in the current climate of protests and police violence around the world, it is important to be sensitive to workshop participants. In order to avoid triggering any negative emotional reactions, I urge leaders to proactively let participants know that the story is about a cop on duty.

My workshops and classes usually run about two hours. If you are leading a session that is well under two hours, see my recommendation in #3 below.

Recipe

OPENING ANNOUNCEMENT

Today's challenge is to draft a narrative that contains a portal of some sort. The portal represents a shift in time, location, or identity, to name only a few transition features. Use a sensation to trigger the portal. For example, I could write about being in this room and my character walks to a window and looks out to see a parade (or a pickpocket, or animals playing, and so on). The story transitions at that point entirely to the new scene, with or without the original character. The story continues in the new scene and does not necessarily return to the original scene. In this example, the view through the window is the literal portal. *Any sensory mode* can be used to prompt a shift in the story.

Note to leader: I try not to provide too many examples of portal transitions, so that participants actively strive to find their own portal device and storyline. In fact, I use the window portal as an obvious example so that the portal idea is understood and the example seems attainable.

STEPS

1. You will have twenty minutes to map out your story. No worries if the story is not complete! Today's workshop is a difficult compositional challenge.

After 20 minutes . . .

2. (*To leader*: Hand out photocopies of Michael Schrider's "17 Years as a Beat Cop" and/or Amelia Farquharson's "Beyond Realism.") Let's read these stories out loud. Who wants to read for us?
3. Discuss. Where's the portal? What observations do you have about the story? How do sensory-rich details contribute to the overall story? How about numbers (in Schrider's story)? Body orientations? Flow?
4. Now that we have read one or two "portal" story examples, let's draft *a new story*. Everyone take another twenty minutes to write.
5. Discuss. If there is time, some participants may like to read their stories or talk about their writing process and transitions. (*To leader*: if your session time is under two hours, I suggest taking on only #1. You can assign the two readings and a two- to five-page "Through the Portal" story for the next meeting time.)

Variation

How might the portal compositional form provide possibilities for other creative endeavors that are not based in literal narrative? For example, music or dance improvisations or compositions could be mapped using a conceptual portal transition, despite the lack of realism.

Ask participants to consider the portal theme for an improvisation or composition. I have been surprised that students find the puzzle interesting and, even better, state they feel empowered to dream up unusual transitions that they might not have considered or had an opportunity to imagine.

Post-Exercise Discussion Topics

Discussion about the form, whether about a short story, a sci-fi movie, or an abstract compositional form, always arises.

Sensory Studies and Fieldwork

"Through the Portal" in sensory studies and fieldwork contexts works surprisingly well. It raises issues about the cultural construction of reality, other realms, and storytelling. Emphasizing the senses as portals is quite a challenge. Workshop participants effusively discuss a wide variety of themes that inspired their sensory examinations. One prominent theme has been the nature of exploring other dimensions and how the portal exploration afforded a consideration of sensory orders beyond the five we are taught in grade school. The idea of cultures "making sense" of the world has arisen as a discussion theme. The exploration also fosters a discussion of different cultures' notion of liminal thresholds, "other worlds," the sense of time (as well as the concept of time), and compositional form.

Creativity

Hands down, "Through the Portal" stands out as one of the favorite challenges in my workshops. Participants often remark that for weeks after the workshop they notice how transitions are used in literature, film, and television shows (especially science fiction!). When participants read one of their short stories to the group the entire room is riveted, hanging on every word to see if they can guess where the portal transition appears. The idea that portals can be triggered by any sensory mode encourages participants to be creative.

Curios

Backstory and Overview

Found objects occupied a great deal of my attention as a child, perhaps to the point of fixation. Miscellaneous odds and ends tossed into toolboxes or unsorted knickknacks at the bottom of a sewing box filled me with curiosity. These curios demanded my close inspection. Mesmerized by these things, I wondered what the objects were and tried "making sense" of how they came to exist next to the other items in the bin.

Preparation (significant)

Collect a wide variety of small objects, preferably ones with unusual appearances, interesting tactile or sonic qualities, different colors, or somewhat puzzling features. I like to select things with character, meaning they have been worn by use, suggest activity and life, and have seen better times. Some examples from my collection: a crushed, teal-colored metal toy car that I found flattened in the street; a tiny gold plastic doll's brush; an old wooden whistle; seashells; a broken brooch, a wooden spool of thread; an embellished brass Indian bell with frayed red string still attached; a dented penny; a glass marble; broken scissors. You get the idea. These objects have been appreciated and display their stories.

FIGURE 5. "Curios."

Place these curios in a shallow box, plate, cigar box, or old tin. I found that a small drawer that must have belonged to a jewelry box worked well for my curio collection. The container provides a bit of mystery itself and helps to prompt some adventure for the exploration.

"Curios" can easily be adapted for a solo writing/drawing prompt, as well as for online prompts. In both cases participants are encouraged to select a found object, preferably one that they do not have prior attachments to. A found item that one comes upon, such as the toy car mentioned above, is ideal.

Recipe

STEPS

1. Everyone form groups of three to five and sit together, but away from the other groups if possible.

2. When I come around to your group, please select one curio for the group. Take a moment to spend time holding and inspecting your curio.
3. I'll give you twenty minutes to write a narrative about the curio or influenced by some aspect of the object. (Depending on the group, participants can be encouraged to draw or include drawing in their narrative.)

After 20 minutes . . .

4. Going around the room, let's see the curio that each group selected. After that, each person will share a synopsis of their story to the entire group. Include what compelled you to write that particular narrative in response to the curio prompt.
5. Discuss. (If there is time, small groups can share their stories or process.)

Note to Leader

Members of each group tend to consult with each other on the selection of their curio as I walk around with the drawer of objects. I appreciate the exchange as it builds group camaraderie; however, I suggest finding ways to provide some sense of urgency so that the selection process itself does not eat up time.

Sensory Studies and Fieldwork

For sensory studies and fieldwork projects, the awareness of objects and their context is valuable. Most importantly, objects can reveal historical and cultural stories that can be used as a means for initiating an interview or even save a seemingly dead-end interview midstream. Allow me to clarify. Bringing a pertinent item to an interview or noticing one at the site is one way to break the ice for conversation. Objects can instantly stimulate memories and associations. During interviews, objects can help to draw the attention of the interlocutor as well as the interviewer, preventing a potentially awkward opening conversation. However, such objects can also be brought in partway through an interview, if there are silent moments that signal the end of a topic or some kind of discomfort on the interlocutor's side. People love to talk about objects! For example, I was interviewing a Monster Truck driver, and the interview seemed to be dwindling and coming to a halt earlier than expected. I noticed a toy Monster Truck stuck under a side table near the couch and asked about it. Soon the discussion moved to a number of fascinating topics I had not anticipated—children attending rallies, gendered toys, his own childhood, play groups, and so on.

Creativity

I marvel at how effortlessly the drawer curios prompt focused attention and fascination. When I place unusual, distressed objects in the drawer, they are immediately selected, and participants say that their stories flow from their intense curiosity about how the item came to appear that way (the flattened toy car, for instance) or as they noticed its tactile qualities ("I never noticed that this common object had ridges"). Similar to a sensory fieldwork session, objects prompt a range of memories and associations for people. In my creativity workshops, participants consistently remark how the same object brought forth contrasting (or similar) memories for members in a group.

Wearables

Backstory and Overview

I will be honest, Halloween continues to be my favorite holiday. It provides a mysterious, mystical evening for kids and adults to imagine themselves as someone or something else. When I was a child, we never *bought* costumes. In fact, just the opposite. Planning and anticipation for the one night where kids in the neighborhood would be allowed out late, in the dark, brought thrilling challenges.

Some costumes took an entire month to build. A memorable one involved working with chicken wire, papier-mâché, and cloth to construct a giant monster head that sat on my shoulders, and I peered out through a gauze-covered hole located under the monster's chin.

"Wearables" offers a compelling challenge for participants. How might a wearable alter or enhance one's identity? While the planning, decision-making, selection of materials, building, and display may appear merely logistical, the process of making tangible the dream of an altered identity truly provides a healthy challenge.

An optional written component can be incorporated. An example by Katherine Tyrol is provided in the "Resources" chapter at the close of the book.

Preparation (minimal)

I offer the workshop participants several bags of assorted materials to work with. If "Wearables" is offered on a college campus, students often do not have materials, so several times during the weeks approaching the due date event I encourage them to let me know what they might need. Some students may need fishing line, fabric, or tools, for example.

Wearables is not an in-class project. I describe the project during a session and provide the deadline. I encourage leaders to provide at least one to three weeks for magnificent results!

Recipe

OPENING ANNOUNCEMENT

Here's your challenge: Create something that you will wear to class. It can be subtle or obvious.

Your wearable needs to be YOUR creation, not a store-bought "costume."

Be creative! Found objects are a terrific challenge. Should you need materials (glue, wire, fishing line, thread, fabric, yarn) or tools, let me know and I'll see if I can supply it.

Rule: *You must wear your wearable into our room*. That means, no arriving to class and then dressing once you are in the room. (At this point I remind the group where the washrooms are in the building.)

On the due date we will have a celebration where everyone has five to ten minutes to display their wearable. Being in character, if appropriate, is encouraged. Codeswitching between identities is welcome (meaning, being in character for a portion of the time, then being "oneself" to explain how you made decisions and built the wearable).

Note to Leader

While "Wearables" fosters a playful side, it can potentially inhibit shy participants. I assign "Wearables" once I know my crowd. For some groups I confidently ramp up the circus-like ambience; for others I reinforce that creating a subtle wearable can offer just as challenging a project. (Examples of subtle wearables: hair ornaments, a macramé bracelet, shoes, an "arm knit" scarf.)

Decide whether the challenge culminates in a short paper reflecting on participants' process, influences, experiences.

Post-Exercise Discussion Topics

"Wearables" is the one exploration where a discussion busts open simply as a result of the hullabaloo and the presence of new identities in the space. Instead of our typical discussion, we have a "group mingle" while celebrating and visiting our new participants. Participants eagerly ask questions about others' wearables and how they constructed them.

Sensory Studies and Fieldwork

Our identities, displayed in a wide range of sensory information (from subtle to dramatic), offer a complex cultural, personal, and sociological mix of life experiences to unpackage. The sensory lessons in "Wearables" may not be apparent upon reading the exploration recipe. But trust me, they certainly reveal themselves. Participants often exclaim how building or rebuilding their identity provides a perspective into themselves and an awareness of how everyone codeswitches and manifests multiple identities through even a single day. I often assign readings pertaining to codeswitching in linguistics, as well as in movement and everyday life (see Hahn and Bahn 2002; Heller 1988). Please do not overlook the potentials for "Wearables" for graduate seminars or workshops for adults. One graduate student, Katherine Tyrol (now a professor), sewed an entire costume and conducted fieldwork at a festival for gamers where attendees often don the full regalia of game characters. She noted that, not being an extrovert by nature, the wearable afforded her the ideal cloak for her ethnographic identity at the site. See her essay in the "Resources" chapter at the close of the book.

Creativity

The "Wearables" exploration pushes creativity to the max. When creativity plays a major role in the design of a workshop, I offer the exploration twice in the semester. During the first meeting I encourage participants to offer potential ways to enhance, improve, or expand upon the project. Then, the group has a week or two to make their second wearable, which *can be* an expanded version of the first.

Me +

Backstory and Overview

I visited museums weekly with my parents as a kid. As artists, they taught me the proportions of the human body in the halls of museums as we looked at paintings and sculpture and also at posters of Leonardo da Vinci's *L'Uomo Vitruviano*. I specifically remember my father's emphatic lectures on the human head and face. He was so animated that I can recall being riveted by the general proportions of the head. For example, when I was eight years old and he said, "The eyes are at the halfway line between the top of the head and chin," the information seemed puzzling. How can that be? Everyone in grade school drew eyes at the top third of the circle at school, after all. But we stood in front of a mirror together and measured with our hands . . . oh, what a surprise! Next, he'd say, "There is an eye-width between our eyes." We took thumb and index finger to span an eye's width, then placed that measurement between our eyes over the bridge of our noses. Magic!

"Me +" presents information about the proportions of the human head at the opening of a workshop, then moves on to an imaginary, creative project of a half mask. The half mask idea is not my own, and I urge you to consider other inspiring half mask ideas (a horizontal half mask, for instance).

FIGURE 6. "Me +": drawing by Safa Koreshi.

FIGURE 7. "Me +": drawing by Katie Boyd.

Learning body proportions begins the exploration; however, "Me +" expands into a creative and identity musing zone quickly. Participants consider notions of identity, alter egos, doppelgängers, superheroes, and their own perspectives.

Note: you do not need to be a visual artist to convey this information. In fact, most often a rough drawing sketched on the board (versus a perfectly executed one) will encourage participants to think, "OK, I can do that." The point here is to encourage everyone to draw and to consider body proportions, other species' proportions, how proportions might reveal humanity, and *how we sense the world.*

Preparation (significant)

A quick search on the internet using "life drawing head proportions" will provide you with plenty of examples. One that I find helpful is "Practicing Drawing Faces Assignment" from Ms. Mack's Art Classroom website: https://sites.google.com/a/pgcps.org/msmack/art-1/portraiture-color-theory-patterned-monochromatic-self-portraits/portraiture-color-theory-project (accessed July 30, 2020). I purposely draw only the rough basics on the whiteboard (see figure 8), but you may want to provide handouts.

Bring paper, pencils, and black markers to the workshop. I use photocopy paper for the sketches but bring in white card stock for the final drawing so it is rigid when taking photographs.

Optional: have a mirror in the room.

Recipe (in Three Parts)

Part A: Mapping Proportions of the Head

OPENING ANNOUNCEMENT

Today we'll study the proportions of the human face, followed by a creative take-home project.

STEPS

1. Please draw in your notebook the proportion guide that I sketch out on the whiteboard. We will do this a few times, so no concerns about the appearance.
2. First, draw an oval or circle. Then draw centered horizontal and vertical dotted guidelines intersecting at the middle. (See figure 8.)
3. Draw three eyes in a row; you may sketch the middle eye lightly or with a dotted line.
4. Let's mark a horizontal guideline halfway between the horizontal line and the chin. This is the base of the nose.

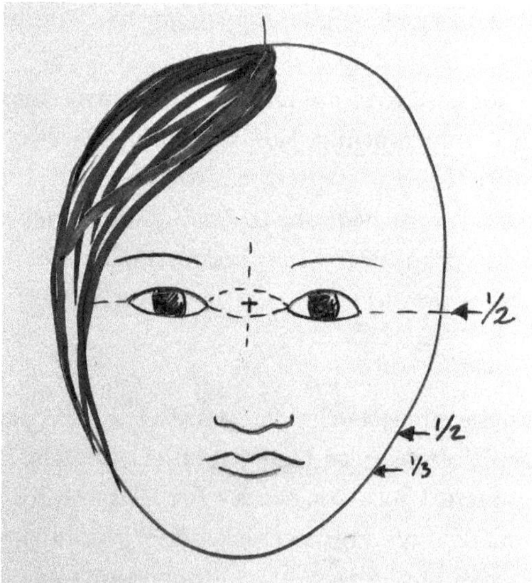

FIGURE 8. Basic proportions of the face, a whiteboard sketch.

5. Divide the space between the base of the nose and the bottom of the chin into thirds. A third of the way down from the base of the nose, draw a horizontal dotted line. This line indicates where the lips come together.

Part B: Creating Proportion Templates (in Three Steps)

STEP 1 (ten–twenty minutes)

a. Set aside your proportion sketches. Everyone take a blank sheet of paper and pair up with a partner. We are going to make face templates and then create a "wacky mask."
b. One person in your team: cover the right or left side of your face with the paper. It is best if the paper is situated so that there is space below your chin and above your head.
c. Your partner will help you position the paper and mark your face guidelines on the template. Take a pencil or marker and put a dash at the chin, center line of the lips, bottom of the nose, midline of the eye, and top of the head.
d. Trade roles so that each person has a personal face template with guidelines. This paper serves only as a template for the next step. (Note: if there is a mirror, adjustments can be made.)
e. Everyone write their names on their template.

STEP 2 (works well as a take-home assignment)

a. Imagine your alter-ego animal (or superhero, bird, insect, monster, or robot, depending on the group).
b. Drawing lightly, transfer your guidelines onto another sheet of paper, keeping the original template guide for other sketches.
c. Draw your animal face so that the face aligns with the guidelines from your own face. (See two examples pictured at the top of the recipe, figures 6 and 7.)

STEP 3

Take photographs!

I enjoy this part of the exploration. It gives me solo time with each participant to plan the shot and chat. If a participant's alter ego has antennae or ears, then I might suggest a pigtail (see figure 7, where Katie used a rubber band to gather up part of her hat to form an ear). If the character has a wild mane, I ask them to tousle their hair. You get the point. Be creative as you are presented with these new identities. The rigidity of cardstock helps because the paper will stand upright.

Part C: Stories and Discussion

Part C is optional. However, if your group embraces storytelling, or writing is an aim of your meetups, "Me +" contributes a terrific multilayered prompt. I find that briefly reminding the group of the previous stages of "Me +" helps everyone to note how far they've gone in a short time.

OPENING ANNOUNCEMENT

Because everyone has created their alter-ego half mask, let's take the time to write about your alter egos. Let's write for twenty minutes.

Some prompts that may help you:

- Why did you choose that particular alter ego? (Or did it choose you?)
- Is there a story, real or fictional, connected to your character?
- Do any thoughts about embodiment arise?
- What was your process of designing your other identity?

Note to Leader

I tend to spend only twenty minutes for Part A, as it provides foundational information to launch Part B. I am more interested in the basic knowledge that Part A imparts and how it gets group members motivated to creatively consider their alternate identity. Part C can be a group discussion, a writing exploration, or both.

I purposely placed the note regarding not displaying perfection at the top of the exploration. I cannot underscore enough the power of a rough (imperfect) sketch (unless the participants are all advanced in life drawing). The participants in my workshops and classes are diverse in backgrounds: engineers, musicians, computer scientists, cognitive scientists, dancers, and artists. The most common statement, sadly, is, "I'm not creative" or "I don't know how to draw."

As a leader, your humble nature encourages them to be modest as well. There's no need to be self-deprecating or sheepish. Leading with clarity and confidence will pay off.

Post-Exercise Discussion Topics

Alongside "I'm not creative" you might also hear, "I had no idea our eyes are in the middle of the head!"

Identity is a big topic of discussion, revealed through stories about what animal, insect, or superhero was selected. The storytelling marvelously encourages curiosity, empathy, and bonding.

Sensory Studies and Fieldwork

"Me +" (like "Wearables") offers alternate identities to be revealed. When I ask participants why they chose a particular character, the responses often flow into storytelling about past experiences, or the nature of their identity, or some kind of resonating feature of the character. We often talk about codeswitching (Heller 1988). If we consider that the senses reach beyond the traditional five and how our identities are multiple and melded with emotions and beliefs, the idea of the sensorium deepens.

Creativity

The notion of expanding one's identity has been captured in the arts for ages. Depending on the workshop, "Me +" can be tailored to suit the group's aims. For example, a group exploring identity issues can delve deeper into historical and theoretical roots of mixed or multiple identities, superheroes, codeswitching, doppelgängers, psychological issues (dissociative identity disorders), animation, or fiction, to name just a few.

I hope my emphasis on modeling modesty as a leader intimates how creativity and experimentation can be encouraged, despite protests from the group (the "I'm not creative" claims). "Me +" offers an opportunity to be incredibly playful and yet have expressive and inspiring creative depth.

Mending, a Recipe for One

Allow me to provide several backstories prior to diving in. Because of potential sensitivities, the "Mending" recipe demands a cautious introduction and some patience from readers.

Backstories 1 and 2

Visiting outdoor Buddhist temple sales is one of my favorite activities in Japan. They can be similar to American rummage sales, where a hodgepodge of common and unusual items are displayed for sale. In 1987 I was admiring a low wooden calligraphy table at a temple in Kyoto. Behind me a voice said, "So beautiful," and I nodded in agreement. I turned to find an elderly Buddhist monk standing behind me, wearing his robes in the blazing sun.

He continued, smiling, "It's been appreciated." Looking back at the table, I noticed nicks, dark splotches, and a black, ring-shaped mark. The stains and nicks stood as a visual embodiment of the table's life to be noticed and "appreciated" (versus sanded, refinished, and made "perfect").

Calling attention to qualities of worn objects or spaces has been a recurring theme for me, specifically in Japanese *okeikogoto* (practice arts) contexts. Such stories often begin with the basic idea of noticing and heightening awareness of a quality, then move to a framing of why it might be important. Recounting a Japanese dance lesson, I wrote this:

> I remember my first dance lesson with Iemoto (Headmaster) Tachibana Yoshie in Tokyo. She took my elbow and led me across the studio, pointing at the impeccably clean wood floor. Nothing seemed unusual. "See these marks . . . ," she said, kneeling down on the floor and still pointing here and there. As I bent down to sit by her side, minute water marks and nicks on the floor's surface came into focus. "Those stains are from all of our sweat and tears here together," she continued, sweeping her arm across the room toward the half-dozen onlooking students. "All these marks are from our hard work together every day—dancing." I looked up from the floor to the students and down to the floor again. My eyes, now wide open, saw how speckled the floor was. . . . In this lesson the message of Iemoto's work ethic was very clear. I realized with awe the magnitude of energy that had been expended on this dance floor. When Iemoto's arm stretched out toward the students, Hatchobori [our studio nickname] became personified for me. Dancing bodies had inscribed these marks on the hard floor, contributing symbolically to the larger representation of the school body, and an instantiation of our strong bonds. The students observing my lesson were only a handful of the many generations of bodies that created these patterns I was kneeling on. I felt included in the group, nervous, yet ready to dance. (Hahn 2007, xiii–xiv)

Backstory 3

Allow me to draw your attention to *kintsugi* ("gold joinery"), a fifteenth-century traditional Japanese technique for mending broken pottery. The technique offers a glimpse into a philosophy that stems from Buddhism. Broken ceramics are mended with gold so the mended seams visibly highlight the life and struggles of the object, in contrast to a mere pragmatic repair. Kelly Richmond-Abdou writes,

> Rather than rejoin ceramic pieces with a camouflaged adhesive, the Kintsugi technique employs a special tree sap lacquer dusted with powdered gold,

> silver, or platinum. Once completed, beautiful seams of gold glint in the conspicuous cracks of ceramic wares, giving a one-of-a-kind appearance to each "repaired" piece.
>
> This unique method celebrates each artifact's unique history by emphasizing its fractures and breaks instead of hiding or disguising them. In fact, Kintsugi often makes the repaired piece even more beautiful than the original, revitalizing it with a new look and giving it a second life. (2019)

The spirit and philosophy of *kintsugi* is worthy of much deeper, lifelong introspection, related to Buddhist philosophical, spiritual, and aesthetic approaches on the frailty of life and existence. If the practice interests you, I highly encourage an online visual search for *kintsugi*, where you will find breathtaking examples of pottery. There are a few books written by psychologists and wellness professionals, emphasizing healing approaches based on more metaphoric themes of *kintsugi*. (See Kumai 2018; Navarro 2018; Santini 2019.) For my purposes here I reference *kintsugi* as one of several influences on the "Mending" recipe, alongside the two backstories above.

Mishaps arise. Sometimes objects we are deeply attached to change . . . a chipped mug, a crushed toy, a torn shirt, a shattered moment, a broken nail, jewelry. All of us have dropped something at some time, watched it shatter, and in the moment exclaimed, "Oh no!" Note that the meditation on the simplest of broken objects penetrates tender spaces in our hearts, bodies, and minds. As metaphors for larger concerns, these thoughts might be difficult to process, not to mention what one might do with the leftover "shards," real, ephemeral, or metaphoric. Also note that I avoid expanding the list to sentient beings that have been injured or departed (such as people and animals). Opening that door would be irresponsible, as it can expose emotions that I do not feel are appropriate for this context. I hope you will choose wisely for your own context, training, and well-being. Because "Mending" appears in a book, devoid of any ongoing interaction or support, I offer the recipe as a contemplative recipe for one. If a literal mending or patching project is not to your liking, see the variation at the close, which can be useful preparation prior to embarking on a larger project.

The theme of "Mending" draws from experiences of things broken, torn, shattered, and misshapen. The recipe requires that a participant acknowledge their concerns about a meaningful object that has broken and consider creative ways of transforming it. Needless to say, transformation represents a process, both physical and emotional. I suggest starting small, reserving time in the future for a broken object that has greater personal meaning for you.

Preparation (significant)

Locate an object that you notice has a blemish or is actually broken. You may need to wait for one to present itself, since we often tend to toss broken objects. Putting an object in the trash bin puts it away from our sensory awareness and, conveniently, the disturbance as well. But how might we reconsider the life of the object? How can we honor its past and present existence? How might we transform it? Mending the object might make it stronger or at the very least different. How can your transformation enhance the fracture, the "mend"?

Broken objects to consider: a broken toy, broken jewelry, a torn shirt, an unraveling sweater, a damaged or torn book.

Recipe

The recipe for "Mending" demands a different approach according to the object you find and who you are. However, the overarching process is simple: locate an object, contemplate its current state, consider the process of transformation, work through the change, continue living with it in its new state. Below, I provide slightly more detailed stages to consider, as well as a few examples.

STEPS

1. Locate an object and contemplate it for *at least* a day without changing it. I suggest displaying the object in some way so you come in contact with it throughout your day. Even better, at the end of a day, take twenty minutes to sit with the object as a contemplation. If you know that focusing on the object in such a way elicits difficult emotions, then you may not be ready to work on that particular piece. If so, set it aside and find something imbued with less weighty emotions. Noticing the difficult emotions can be half the work.
2. See if you can dream up at least five ways to transform the object, however whimsical. How can you breathe new life into this object? Ask yourself if you are capable (technically) to take on the project. Write and sketch the ideas onto paper. The process helps to solidify your intentions, and you might be surprised that other ideas spring to life. After a period of consideration, decide which transformation design you will work on.

3. Consider what tools, supplies, and techniques you will need. Will you require assistance from someone?
4. Embark on the project. However, take your time—the process might be more valuable than the outcome.
5. Live with the object as a new entity. Display it.
6. Optional: write and/or draw about the experience. Even better, keep a journal that documents your creative process. Include why you chose the particular piece, your attachments, your decision-making, how you actively transformed the object, the outcome, and how you feel about the process. Because "Mending" is a recipe for one, you may find that writing helps to process a wealth of thoughts and emotions. Some people find it helpful to share their experience with others by telling the story of the life of the original object, how it broke, and then how it was transformed.

Mending Example

When my mother passed away, my sister and I packed some of her belongings. One lovely find was her childhood kimono. Now, after close to ninety years, the silk was torn in a few places yet retained its beautiful design and of course its sentimental value. A simple sewing project helped me to transform the fabric into two long scarves for Kimiko and myself. Handling the fabric, disassembling the kimono, sewing, and giving the scarf to my sister rooted me in contemplative ways and helped me to process more than the project before me.

Mending Variation: Memories

Merely recalling a scenario when an object that you cared about broke can generate a powerful and transformative experience. Visualize it in as much sensory detail as possible. Write about it. Draw it. Can you remember how you first received (or created) the object? How you used it or displayed it before it broke? Depending on what the object is, the storyline and memory will vary greatly. Even if you ended up tossing or losing the item, there are many possibilities to process and provide an ending, or closure, to your story. For example, if appropriate, can you creatively imagine the (fictional) existence of the object? After you threw it away in the dumpster, it ended up rolling out of the garbage truck and down the road, and a puppy ran off with it . . . (you get the picture!). In other cases, you may know where the object resides but cannot access it. How might you write about it in its current state?

Mending Variation: Suggested Reading and Writing Prompts

Kyoko Nakajima's "When My Wife Was a Shiitake" is a tender short story that conveys a number of cultural sentiments, including mending (one's heart), recipes, cooking, nostalgia, loss, and memory. The story pairs well with "Mending" and as preparation for the following writing prompts. See https://www.wordswithoutborders.org/article/when-my-wife-was-a-shiitake (accessed August 30, 2020).

Mending Writing Prompts

Consider the following list of words. Select one for a writing prompt and see where it takes you: enhance, patch, shatter, wreck, accept, rip, break, slit, defect, hurt, smash, fragment, crash, resilience, hole, stain, mend, overhaul, disaster, remedy, improve, raise, busted, snap, gut, deface, refurbish, darn, transform, recover, torn, burst, revive, demolish, strengthen, mangle, rejuvenate, correct, splice, collapse, split, crush, scrape, transform, change, repair.

Dictionary Ritual

Backstory and Overview

Upon spying a stack of dictionaries in a recycling dumpster, I didn't hesitate to snatch up a beautiful, weathered hardbound copy. The book was worn from use yet sturdy, and it included index notches, the indented cutouts on the side of the book at the start of each section of a dictionary. The spark for a workshop recipe came to me right at the dumpster site.

This recipe is in the form of a ritual. Participants sit in small groups of three or four and perform a word selection "ritual" with the leader. Groups find the ritual format intriguing and enjoyable, especially because each participant has a role to play. Collaboration and independent work follow, closing with a group discussion to share participants' themes. If there is extra time, a larger group discussion works well.

Consider a ritual in your life. How might sensory information help to structure a ritual? For example, is sound or smell incorporated as a mnemonic device? Or as a means of signaling different sections of a ritual? Do sensory details of a ritual provide long-term memories for a group?

Preparation (moderate)

Leaders need a (preferably used) dictionary and a bamboo skewer (in a pinch a sharp pencil will suffice). Optional: a pair of scissors or plastic box cutter. If a recycled dictionary is not available, any (nonreligious or spiritual) used book will serve well.

Recipe

OPENING ANNOUNCEMENT

Please take out your notebooks and writing implements. Form groups of three or four participants. I will be coming around to each group with a dictionary to perform a ritual with your group.

Here are the stages . . .

STEPS

1. The first person will be handed a bamboo skewer and will insert it into the dictionary in a random location. I will open the dictionary to those pages.
2. The second person will choose one of the two pages that have been selected. You may want to glance at the front and back of each of the two pages.
3. The third person rips or cuts the page out of the dictionary. No worries! I literally saved this dictionary from a recycling bin. You are giving it a new life with your creative work.
4. Person four (or the group) selects one word or picture from one of the pages for the group. The same word is used as a prompt for all members.
5. Once the word is selected, no talking. Your chosen word or picture is your group's prompt. Now freewrite and/or draw for ten minutes. I'll let you know when time is up.
6. Discuss. Please share with your group as much as you would like to about your writing or drawing. You need not read your writing out loud, but do share two features: (a) how the dictionary prompt was incorporated into your work, and (b) your writing/drawing process, even if it is merely to say that you had difficulties or that your mind and story wandered.

Note to Leader

Now and then a student will raise concerns about the disrespectful act of desecrating a book. Be sure to let the group know early in the session that you care about books, that the text had been tossed out, and that their ritual is actually breathing new life into the book.

The small group talks are essential, particularly to instill the values of attentive listening. Encourage curiosity. Participants bond a great deal as a result. For example, if "leopard" was selected as the prompt word, a group member might write a short story about a leopard's roar, another may freewrite about a leopard's spots and then meander into issues concerning identity or a personal reflection about a childhood stuffed animal, while another may write about the fur industry and animal rights. These leopard scenarios were actual examples from a workshop. My point here is that the sharing of their freewrite scenes and how they arrived at their narrative is an important aspect of the workshop.

Post-Exercise Discussion Topics

Groups often marvel at the similarities and differences of each participant's story or drawing. It is common for a room of thirty participants (divided into ten groups) to animatedly, even loudly, connect with each other while talking about their work. I appreciate it when a room comes alive like this.

How and why participants collaboratively selected their word can bond the group. When individual groups speak to the larger workshop gathering, I notice that their collective group story becomes a source of pride—in a sense, a meta-story.

Discussions about what rituals are and how the recipe afforded different kinds of interactions among the participants often are raised.

Sensory Studies and Fieldwork

"Dictionary Ritual" incorporates several fieldwork-like scenarios. The use of a mock ritual format kindles questions about what a ritual is and how being a member of a small group performing a ritual might impact one's expressive output and interactions. If ritual is a central focus of the workshop, I always bring a bell and ring it to signal the opening and closing of each small group ritual. Readings or a short talk on ritual or ritual studies, with ample examples, pairs well with "Dictionary Ritual" (for starters, see Bell [1992] 2009; Bell 2009; Shelemay 2015). I ask the group how various sensory modalities might structure, enhance, or deepen a ritual. Ask for examples they know. If they need prompting, I will ask about specific sound cues, movements, or smells such as incense to get the discussion started. The recipe includes several layers of social interaction: formation of the group identity during the word selection process; members' collaboration; listening to each other; the larger group discussion. I find the attentive listening and observation reinforces the type of heightened attention needed when interviewing people in the field or observing a scene of participants and the environment.

Creativity

Groups meeting for creative purposes eagerly consume "Dictionary Ritual," pushing themselves individually and as small groups. How the prompt word or picture inspires and then develops into an expressive piece can be wildly creative. During discussions, especially if their group partners inspire and support each other's writing and drawings, participants have even requested to return to their freewriting/drawing to expand or make edits. The "finished" products develop from these discussions and input.

Sell It

Overview

"Sell It" challenges participants to sell the group on *something*. Basically, the exploration asks participants to create a commercial for something. What are the elements that support a good sale? I use "Sell It" as an opportunity to push everyone to go over the top, whether it's serious rhetoric, management, comic sales pitch voices, parody, fake products, kitsch—all can be part of the exploration. The point is to push to a point of silliness or bombast, then have a group critique of real-world issues that compose a sale.

For example, have you ever had an image or jingle stuck in your mind? Sometimes referred to as earworms, catchy songs feel like they take over mental space. But what happens when it's a lasting or repeating image or other sensory impression that just won't go away? All forms of media take advantage of these phenomena to impose their commercials into your daily life. How might we examine sales through the lens of sensory awareness? Memory? Psychology? (For an interesting case, see Jakubowski et al. 2017.)

"Sell It" works well as a group activity. Different participants can design the visuals, write the text, be actors, design props, and provide sound effects or music. "Sell It" can easily be assigned for an online class. In fact, it can add an upbeat playfulness to an online class. The participant or small group needs to design a project as a commercial for presentation to the larger group.

Preparation (moderate)

I find it helpful to select a few examples of commercials from television, social media, newspapers, or magazines and bring them to the session for discussion. Commercials from different eras offer particularly interesting historical analysis, not to mention jovial conversations about products past and present. Even better, ask participants to bring in several examples to share.

Recipe

OPENING ANNOUNCEMENT

Today we will focus on attracting the attention of an audience to sell something. You will be gathered into groups to design a one- to two-minute "commercial." Imagine a street barker or an actor/writer for a television advertisement or radio commercial. How does that actor attract viewers' attention? What is the lure? The hook?

The key is to sell the group something through a thickly described sensory landscape. One needs to consider "over-the-top" or superlative ways of writing (ways of conveying what you are selling from an experience, a product, food, and so on).

STEPS

1. Form groups of three to five people and sit together.
2. You will have ten to twenty minutes to discuss the basics. What will you sell? It does not need to be an object; it could be an experience or activity.
3. Decide collaboratively who will be responsible for each aspect of the "commercial" and be sure to continue to work collaboratively so all of the various parts enhance and support the sell.

4. The commercial is limited to one to two minutes and should be repeatable. (Here the leader can decide a specific time or whether a longer infomercial style is best for the group.)
5. Present all of the works.
6. Discuss.

Note to Leader

I find the pressure of the ninety-minute workshop to create a commercial helps the group move along. However, the exploration can also be assigned on one day and then presented in the next session, especially if your meeting time is only one hour.

Post-Exercise Discussion Topics

Participants often say they notice the form and style of commercials, magazines, and social media sales tactics in everyday life after the exploration.

Sensory Studies and Fieldwork

Commercials vary greatly across cultures, as do products and the kinds of media used to sell products or experiences. Awareness of the compositional form and the sensory nature of sales tactics can raise fascinating cultural issues and value systems. For example, a subtle palette of color for a television commercial or the presence of flowers may hint toward a particular mood or sensory field, even if (for example) scent is not actually transmitted by the commercial.

Creativity

"Sell It" can be stretched in any direction you like. In one class, I had a group that wanted to be more performative, while another group wanted to create a visual design for a billboard on the highway. The discussion afterward raised interesting issues around presence and how to draw people's attention in different contexts.

Hybrid-o-phones

Overview

What better way to contemplate sound-producing instruments than having participants build their own? I set aside a portion of a class (or several classes if the group focuses on music) to introduce the physics of sound, what a musical instrument is, how ethnomusicologists classify instruments across cultures, and the Sachs-Hornbostel classification system, and then I problematize classification systems (Schaeffner 2016a, 2016b; DeVale 1990).

Preparation (considerable)

The recipe can be conducted over several sessions. The organology talk can be delivered on the first meeting, followed by a project assignment to be built outside of class. The project is to create a "hybrid-o-phone" (a fictitious category!) from found materials. Participants learn about basic organology and classifications, musicology and ethnomusicology, culture, materials, sensory aspects of hearing versus listening, and creativity.

Classifying Musical Instruments: The Basics

Different cultures classify musical instruments in a variety of ways. Ethnomusicologists have incorporated and adapted the Sachs-Hornbostel (S-H) system to find a holistic way to uniformly classify instruments across cultures according to how the instrument produces sound—that is, how vibrations are set into motion. The classification system was created by Curt Sachs and Erich Moritz von Hornbostel (originally published in 1914) and included four basic categories. Later, a fifth category, "Electrophones," was added to incorporate contemporary instruments that produced sound with electricity. In practice, ethnomusicologists incorporate the S-H system for classification while also acknowledging a culture's particular system of classification. Below are the bare bones of the S-H classification system. See also the online OnMusic Dictionary entry for the system: https://dictionary.onmusic.org/terms/1731-hornbostel-sachs (accessed September 30, 2020).

I encourage workshop leaders to bring in instruments for each category, show photographs, play music, show videos of the instruments in the various categories, and offer readings that will fit your group's focus. For some classes I spend nearly one session on each category to really unpackage the material and to spend time listening to instruments and viewing the diversity of playing techniques across cultures. Below, I include the etymology of the terms, which participants find insightful.

The "Phone" Categories

The Greek root "phon" means "sound."

But before I state this, I invite participants to ponder what the root "phone" means. After "sound" is identified, I ask for other instances where "phone" appears as part of a word (symphony, megaphone, phonetic, phonograph, and cacophony are a few, for starters).

Categories

1. Idiophones

   Idios: Greek for "own," "personal," "distinct" (see definition online at https://en.oxforddictionaries.com/definition/idio-, accessed 6/30/2019).

   These are *self-sounding sound* makers. I point out that the word "idiophone" identifies why the instruments in this category are grouped together. Idiophones are instruments made of naturally sonorous materials not needing any additional tension (such as strings or drumskins). The basic question is how the instruments are set into vibration. Examples are rattles, bells, and cymbals.

2. Aerophones

   Aēr: Greek for "air" (see definition online at https://www.lexico.com/en/definition/aero-, accessed 6/30/2019).

   Aerophones include what are usually called "wind instruments." There are two essential factors to sound production: a tube enclosing a column of air, and a device for setting that air into vibration. There are a few instruments with a different acoustical principle called free aerophones, such as bull-roarers.

3. Membranophones

   Membrana: Latin for "limb," "membrane," "surface" (see definition online at https://www.etymonline.com/word/membrane, accessed 6/30/2019).

   Membranophones produce sound by stretching a membrane over an opening. Most, but not all, membranophones are called drums.

4. Chordophones

   Cord and *chorda*: Latin for "chord" or "rope"; *cord*: Greek khordē, "gut," string of a musical instrument. (See https://www.lexico.com/en/definition/cord, accessed 6/30/2019.)

Chordophones are instruments with strings. The number of stringed instruments can be reduced to four fundamental subcategories, organized by the shape and orientation of the strings to the resonating body, or sound board. Here is a very general overview: *lutes* (have necks and the strings run parallel to the neck and resonating body); *zithers* (the strings run parallel to the resonating body, but zithers do not have a neck); *harps* (strings are vertical to the sound board); and *lyres* (have two armatures and a crossbar; the strings run parallel to the resonating body).

5. Electrophones

   Instruments in which vibrations are produced mechanically or reproduced mechanically.

Recipe

OPENING ANNOUNCEMENT

We have discussed the five traditional categories of musical instruments, particularly the nature of individual timbres or "qualities" of instruments.

The exploration challenge is for everyone to use *found materials* to create a fictitious instrument that spans *at least* TWO of the "-phone" categories, hence the title "HYBRID-o-phones" for the exploration. (Note that "hybrid-o-phone" is not an official category.) "Found materials" means you do not take a preexisting musical instrument and merely modify it (while that is an interesting endeavor, it is not the challenge). The resulting hybrid instrument will be idiosyncratic and entirely your own.

ASSIGNMENT REQUIREMENTS

- Your hybrid-o-phone needs to be playable!
- *Name it!* Even if you name it "Molly," it needs a name.
- Everyone will introduce and demonstrate their instrument in class. Come prepared to briefly talk about it and play it (three minutes maximum).
- Creativity and ingenuity is key!
- Extra points for performing a brief piece on your instrument.
- Extra points for decorating your hybrid-o-phone.

After everyone has introduced and played their instrument, we will gather into smaller groups to improvise.

Optional

Write a fictional short story about the hybrid-o-phone. For starters, consider: What subculture does the instrument come from? When was it played (for example, is it from a fictive archaeological dig, or from the future)? Who plays the instrument (class, gender, age)? When is the instrument played and for what occasion (ritual, entertainment, personal reflection)?

Sensory Studies and Fieldwork

Considering what the notion of what a category is and why a culture would categorize objects opens up fascinating discussions. Because instruments are created to make sound, have functional and culture-sensitive tactile properties, and often have interesting visual attributes, the sensory modalities expand beyond their sonic capabilities. Sensory studies and ethnomusicology participants often discuss a variety of cultural considerations about instruments in general, such as the context and role an instrument performs in a culture, gendered instruments, performance practices, who is allowed to play an instrument, and secular and sacred instrument traditions.

Creativity

Crafting a fictitious instrument is challenging! Ultimately, the instrument will need to make sound, the performer's body must interface with the instrument somehow, the pragmatic and visual look must be designed, and the builder needs to practice enough so that at minimum he or she can demonstrate the instrument's qualities and preferably be able to improvise with other participants in a free improvisation. The combination of designing a functional instrument that fulfills all of these requirements and spans two instrument categories is a demanding, creative challenge. Because the hybrid-o-phone is fictitious, there is room for wildly creative experimentation both in design and in improvisation.

The Art of Following

There are two versions of "The Art of Following." Each focuses on an array of sensory modalities: moving, with some sonic features (involves visual, kinesthetic, sonic awareness), listening, and tactile. Both heighten sensory awareness of energy flow, transmission, and presence.

Many activities are transmitted directly through demonstration, or active mirroring of a practice. The key to practicing any art through following resides in a development of keen awareness and focus so one can develop sensory memory and duplicate the activity later.

Activities that are learned through demonstration vary widely and range from pragmatic activities and sports to creative arts purposes. I often begin a session by asking the group to provide examples. Interesting ones arise, such as cooking, cleaning a knife properly, tying shoelaces, doing laundry, calligraphy, dance, medical care instructions, woodworking, tying a necktie, martial arts, and billiards. As an aside, I find the examples that individuals raise provide marvelous insights into the character of the group.

The degree to which exact mirroring or duplication of the teacher's practice varies greatly, depending on the culture, the particular activity, and the degree of nuance afforded by the practice.

I propose that *following* is an art form. The process requires absolute focus on multiple sensory modalities. "The Art of Following" recipes raise numerous thematic issues—vicarious experience, empathy, mirroring, accountability, bonding, direct transmission, and control, to name a few.

Growing up, I learned Japanese dance and several *okeikogoto*, such as tea ceremony, flower arrangement, and brush painting. Consuming knowledge in such a way was a part of everyday life. Many *okeikogoto* are considered living arts, meaning the art is passed down and endures through the embodied transmission from teacher to student. Transmission practices, as a result, can be quite strict, because a disciplined practice ensures appropriate enculturated embodiment and the lived legacy of the tradition.

Learning through doing demands "single-pointed" focus, a process of study rooted in meditation and other Japanese cultural practices. Fascinated by how knowledge is transmitted and embodied in different cultures, I devoted my doctoral research to sensory transmission (published in 2007 as *Sensational Knowledge: Embodying Culture through Japanese Dance*). Years later, "The Art of Following" exploration emerged while considering two general areas: embodiment via the senses and via creativity.

While the exploration can be playful and quite enjoyable, the practice delves deeply into relationships between people in profound ways—the bonding, empathy, and vicarious experiences that emerge from closeness with another person and even focusing single-pointedly on *being* that person, if only for a moment. In tandem, the dynamics of power structures loom, making the exercise an activity that fosters important conversations on will, tradition, culture, persistence, and empathy.

The Art of Following—Movement, Sound, Presence

Preparation (little to none)

The only requirement is an open space that participants can move in. A large space is not necessary.

Recipe (in Three Parts)

As in previous multipart recipes, the various parts can be carried out in different sessions, or the leader can decide to offer only one.

Part A: Movement Explorations

OPENING ANNOUNCEMENT

Please pair up with a partner. One person will play the leader role first, the other the follower. Later the roles will be switched.

Everyone will learn a short phrase today, and then in our next session you will "perform" the phrase you learned.

(*Note to leader*: The idea of needing to retain what is learned through following exerts just enough pressure on everyone to focus, attend, and retain.)

STEPS

1. Leader (role): Create a brief movement phrase to teach your partner. Commit to a clearly executable sequence of movements *that you can repeat*. Tips: Select a relatively simple phrase but one that has detail. A sequence could be abstract or a pantomime of an activity, such as unlatching and opening a window, or brushing teeth, or opening a carton of milk. Abstractions of an activity are welcome. Be sure to repeat the phrase as closely as possible. The phrase can be a gesture of arms only, or full-bodied.
2. Follower: Stand behind and slightly to the right of your leader, facing in the same direction. The position offers an over-the-shoulder perspective of the phrase, but also can be alternated with different

perspectives. Depending on the phrase, it might be appropriate for the leader to sit while the follower stands. After the first iteration, alternate leader-follower positions can be introduced.

3. *Without speaking*, the leader guides the follower through the sequence. Stop. Repeat at least three to five times.
4. After the lesson, all partners face one other, and the follower repeats the sequence *without guidance*. Should the follower need a "refresher," then make an agreed-upon hand signal (*reminder, there is no talking*), and both leader and follower return to step #2 above.
5. Lift the veil of silence and have a discussion.
6. Switch roles.

Part B: Following with Sound

STEPS

1. Return to the first leader in Part A above.
2. This time the leader adds a vocalization, a sound element, to the original phrase. It need not be the sound effects that narrate the action. In fact, it may be more challenging if the vocalization has a more intricate and contrasting relationship to the movements.
3. Repeat the leader-follower sequence, but this time with movements *and* sounds.

Part C: Sound Accompaniments

(Note: I normally offer Part C in the next session)

OPENING ANNOUNCEMENT

Let's take a different approach to the "art of following," one that has a playful, creative angle. Last time, leaders vocalized their own movements. This round, followers will supply the sounds.

STEPS

1. Everyone create a *new* movement to be used for a following sequence. Try a full-bodied movement exploration phrase, abstract or pantomimed.
2. This time, leader and follower stand facing each other, about three to five feet away from each other.
3. The leader performs the new movement phrase (without sound) as the follower observes. Follower, imagine what kinds of verbal sounds you can make to accompany the movement. Your sounds need not be realistic or even coordinate exactly with the movement. However, the vocalization will need to be repeatable for the next stage.

4. Repeat the movement-sound passage at least five times, with the follower vocalizing after the first iteration.
5. Switch roles.
6. Write in your journal; then discuss.

Optional: Performing

I find that "performing" these short passages of great benefit. One of the most enjoyable, positive experiences was an entire group, lined up, performing in rapid succession so that the entire group performed all of the sequences fluidly as one long phrase. The room filled with giggles, yet the playfulness relaxed everyone and the discussion afterward produced a flurry of productive topics.

Note to Leader

For emphasis on embodying cultural knowledge, I link several sessions that are culturally pertinent to "The Art of Following" exploration. Because I play shakuhachi (Japanese bamboo flute) and also perform Japanese traditional dance, I incorporate "mock" lessons prior to introducing these explorations so that participants can physically experience the feeling of a master-disciple relationship within a particular cultural context—specifically, how serious and difficult the transmission of a living artform can be. Following such mock lessons, I am able to loosen the transmission process to the above exploration.

Depending on the group's focus, sometimes I include a brief talk on the art of Foley effects, or the creation of sound effects (generally for film, animation, and theater work). Participants are always fascinated by Foley effects in kung fu and animation excerpts.

Post-Exercise Discussion Topics

Participants comment on how difficult the process of following is yet also how much fun they are having, despite the challenge. I always ask participants to write about the embodied themes that arose for them, informally in journals or in an assigned essay format. Their writings always include some sort of reflection on a system of learning that they have experienced, often from their childhood. In addition, some profound issues arise about embodied learning, and it is healthy to provide ample time for discussion on such matters.

Sensory Studies and Fieldwork

"The Art of Following" can easily be incorporated into an introduction to sensory studies and fieldwork. In my experience, participants find the exploration deeply insightful when paired with traditional "mock" lessons (see "Note to Leader" section above). The attempt to follow someone else in movement and sound provides a number of sensory and empathic themes that set up important insights for participants planning to conduct fieldwork. The topic of mirror neurons in cognition is also one that can be taken up, if appropriate to the group.

"The Art of Following" activity has the potential to raise issues concerning energy, flow, or presence as a sensory modality. Here is an opportunity to offer that the concept of energy flow (inside and outside the body) is culturally constructed and deeply tied into belief systems. Most people are aware of at least one: the Chinese concept of chi, Japanese ki, or Indian yogic prana, for example. How might we learn about and embody such belief systems *as part of* our sensory fieldwork?

Creativity

You can fold "The Art of Following" into most any workshop or course. If the group generally sits for the duration of their workshop or semester, then adding an exploration that is active helps enormously. Emphasizing how a single-pointed focus promotes flow experiences and deep, embodied understandings clarifies the intention of the recipe. The creative and zany nature of this recipe can playfully loosen up a group with different kinds of experiences and discussions.

The Art of Following—Tactile

Backstory and Overview

Remember playing telephone as a youngster? Did you participate in a tactile version, where kids paired up and drew large letters on someone's back to spell words? I adored the game. The tactile version of "The Art of Following" requires the group to be divided into pairs where one person receives a brief tactile impression, or phrase, mapped on their back, shoulders, and arms. Part B requires an *abstract* phrase, meaning no drawings or letters of the alphabet (despite my backstory above). The important point is for the sequence and quality of the tactile sensory phrase to be perceived, then reproduced. The exploration seems simple, but don't be fooled; a number of compelling insights can arise.

Preparation (little to none)

The leader needs to be sure there is enough space in the room so that pairs can be created. Also, be aware if touching of the back is an issue for participants in your setting.

Recipe (in Two Parts)

Part A: Warm-Up

OPENING ANNOUNCEMENT

The skin is the largest organ of the body. Today's exploration involves the sense of touch on the back, shoulders, and arms.

The sense of touch is particularly interesting because of its complexity. Touch is cutaneous, or of the skin, yet we are able to discern a wide array of qualities, such as pressure, temperature, timing, location, rhythm, direction of flow of the touch, features of the touch (wood, metal, liquid, and so on), and all simultaneously.

Because of the complexity, let's start simple!

STEPS

1. Find a partner and decide who will lead and who will receive this round.
2. Leaders: draw a sequence of large letters one at a time on the receiver's back to create a word. Please refrain from talking.
3. Receivers: tell the leader what you believe the word is.
4. Switch roles and repeat.

Part B: The Challenge

STEPS

1. Return to the first leader and receiver roles. Again, please refrain from talking.
2. Leaders: create a very simple **abstract** tactile phrase. "Draw" the phrase on your partner's back (you can include arms and shoulders if your partner agrees). "Abstract" means no drawings or letters of the alphabet. (For example: long horizontal dash followed by three taps on alternate shoulders, then an outward spiral.)

3. Receivers: if you need to, ask the leader to repeat the phrase until you can replicate the sequence on the leader's back.
4. Receivers: notate the abstract design in your notebook.
5. Switch roles, so leaders are now the receivers, and repeat.
6. Discuss with entire group.

Optional

If there is time, repeat, but with more complex and longer phrases. Add nuances to the wide varieties of qualities, such as a phrase that includes varying pressure in a stroke or rhythmic passages. For example, draw a line from one shoulder to the other across the back, but change the pressure along the way. Follow this stroke with a rhythmic tapping of triplets near the scapula or upper arms, then with a very subtle, light touch with the full palm between the scapula, and so on.

Note to Leader

I make sure I know my group well before introducing this exploration. Naturally, there will be giggles from uneasiness. However, I notice that participants become more serious when tasked to recall the phrase. I always announce that if any are not comfortable joining the exploration, they can act as group observers and take notes.

Post-Exercise Discussion Topics

How wonderful to observe the group having fun with the exploration but then realizing how challenging tactile memory and vocabulary can be! Participants consistently say they had to work diligently to create a phrase but then also to recall the phrase. The leader and follower roles are important to include for the session. Nuances and tactile qualities, such as pressure or timing, are often part of the discussion.

Sensory Studies and Fieldwork

Unless one is a massage therapist or ballroom dance teacher, tactile sequential memory is generally not part of our everyday sensory awareness vocabulary. However, in everyday life we do incorporate tactile memory much more than we realize. Requiring participants to remember a tactile phrase with all of the sequential and nuanced complexities can be a profound insight into sensory modalities and culture.

Creativity

In many ways the creativity in the "The Art of Following—Tactile" exploration resides in building the tactile phrase, almost as if it is a musical or dance phrase. The creativity of incorporating the nuances and varied qualities simultaneously challenges everyone.

Recipe as Form

Overview

"Recipe as Form" invites participants to compose a one- to two-page recipe, considering the organizational structure of a procedure and how the structural form reveals an author's intentions. The exploration works well as a take-home assignment but can be started in a group workshop. Depending on the group, "Recipe as Form" can include other media such as DIY video or audio instructions, storyboards, and graphics. If the senses are an important aspect of your class or workshop, emphasize how the stages of a recipe include sensory cues.

Preparation (moderate)

Collect diverse examples of recipes and other procedures—from cooking, woodworking, exercise, and knitting to walking directions from one location to another, technical specifications from a manual, and first aid instructions.

In some instances, I ask everyone to bring in two recipes or procedures for day one, and we examine the structural formats.

Recipe

OPENING ANNOUNCEMENT

Today we will be studying a variety of recipes or procedures for making or doing something. Your challenge for our next meeting is to create a recipe. Heads up: you'll be swapping your recipe with someone in the group for feedback and discussion.

But first, what is a recipe? The Merriam-Webster Dictionary online defines it as a "prescription," a "set of instructions for making something from various ingredients," or a "formula or procedure for doing or attaining something" (https://www.merriam-webster.com/dictionary/recipe, accessed August 30, 2020). So, if "recipe" does not jibe with you, replace it with another synonym such as "formula," "prescription," "directions," "instructions," "procedure," "process," or "method." The basic idea is to craft a series of steps for someone else to create or do something. Because recipes require an understanding of the sequential form of a process, consideration of the necessary information and ordering of the steps is one of the challenges.

The form of a recipe reveals a great deal. Consider the conceptual approach when addressing notions of notation and order. We recognize notation as a process for remembering knowledge, for prescribing a process and order for replicating an activity. If baking a cake is your desired outcome, then following the recipe will be important. On the other hand, if the point of a recipe is to focus on the process and the outcome is quite flexible, then the recipe can be constructed quite differently. Put another way, one needs to write a recipe with great clarity if the desired outcome is specific. For example, if one wants a group to make or do something specific, with a particular outcome, then the recipe will need to be explicit and strictly ordered. If your recipe results in a functional three-legged chair, for example, then the instructions probably require clear steps. On the other hand, if the intention is to emphasize a process of exploration and not a specific result (a cake or a three-legged chair), then the recipe calls for a different approach, instructional form, and language.

STEPS

1. Please take out your notebooks and draft a few ideas for what recipe or procedure you will take on. Is there a specific outcome? Or would you like to process an experience? Jot down a list of ideas.
2. For our next session, write a one- to two-page recipe or procedure. Be concise and clear. Consider the compositional form and how it might affect the results. Bring in at least two printouts of your recipe.
3. (Next session) Everyone gather into small groups and share your recipes. After at least five to ten minutes, offer some constructive, supportive comments and questions.
4. Discuss as a group.

Note to Leader

I often take the opportunity to provide ground rules for giving feedback. It is well worth the time and effort! I ask everyone to attempt to be as empathetic as possible. While we want to support others' progress and the development of their work with our observations, we also want to be sensitive to how much direction and feedback they might be able to take in at the moment. Because each person is different, live feedback via questions and discussion can serve as a way to warm up and observe how the other person responds. Understandably, if someone put time and effort into creating something, then that person might be quite sensitive to feedback.

A few thoughts: Emphasize that *the feedback is not criticism*. In my workshops I establish feedback as a gift. Ask the observer (person providing feedback) to describe their sensory experience of the work, then move to questions. Meanwhile, ask the person who created the work to have their journal out and, if pertinent, take a few notes. The scenario can be one of mutual respect, not criticism.

Post-Exercise Discussion Topics

Consistently, discussions center around intention and how the compositional form reveals the nature of the task or experience. How much detail to include for a recipe can be a lively topic.

Sensory Studies and Fieldwork

"Recipe as Form" supports sensory fieldwork in several ways. Because recipes impart a time-based presentation and deliberately mapped experience, participants notice instructional ordering and time variables specifically related to sensory modalities. For example, if the recipe entails folding paper, the author needs to recreate the process for the audience. In the case of folding paper, the author may actually take a piece of paper and make the first fold, write about that step, and then move on to the next step, and so on. Conveying the "feel" of the process, actually inhabiting the practice in order to communicate, offers many sensory-rich experiential opportunities to transmit. Also, it is interesting to note assumptions. Which instructions and ingredients are assumed by a subculture and are left out of a recipe? For outsiders, contextualizing "translations" might be necessary.

Creativity

Imparting clearly written or drawn, pragmatic, logical stages in the composition of a recipe presents a challenge for participants. What steps and how much detail is necessary (or too much)? What sensory knowledge and descriptions are vital to complete a recipe—those involving visuals, movement, taste, and smell, to name a few? To raise the creativity level, encourage participants to include graphic storyboards, DIY videos, or audio files.

5
ON THE GO

The following recipes are intended to be easy to grasp and deliver, for those days when you need something on the go.

One Word

One-word prompts have been a classic way of initiating freewriting, free-drawing, and art making. I have a few that have become favorites over the years. Many of the words play upon the sounds of the spoken word, so participants can interpret their meaning for themselves. Here are a few to get you started:

Light
Still
Spirit
Sell / Cell
Eight / Ate
Pique / Peek / Peak
Spell

Fragmented Openings

An unfinished opening line can be an interesting challenge. I ask group members to continue the sentence or incorporate the passage within their text. It can be a nice collaborative exchange as well, if a group is paired up and each participant provides a fragment for a partner. Please consider "borrowing" from your favorite authors as well!

A few examples:

"We tell ourselves . . ."

"She turned to me and said . . ."

"There is nothing more . . ."

Boundaries and Limitations

Word Limitations

Write a passage, limiting the word count to a specific number. I tend to enjoy meaningful, auspicious numbers that demand attention and focus. Try 6, 88, 99, or 108.

As a bet with his colleagues, Ernest Hemingway allegedly composed a complete story with six words: "For sale: baby shoes, never worn." Urban legend or not, the concept for the prompt provides a marvelous six-word challenge.

Location Limits

1. Describe an object in the room in as much detail as possible.
2. Repeat. This time, limit the selection of the object to a particular location, such as an object located at or below six inches from the floor or on the ceiling.
3. Describe a sound that resonates from outside the room in as much detail as possible.

Mystery Box

Bring a box to your workshop (2′ x 2′ x 2′ works well). Sit on the floor next to it until the chatter in the room quiets. Notice the box and turn your attention to it in a focused way. Slowly open it and peer in. Be performative and mysterious!

Optional: place materials in the box that make sound, such as plastic bags and paper. Reach in and create sound, but do not reveal what the objects are.

Close the lid. Smile. Ask everyone to write and/or draw about their experience of the event.

Sound and Memory

Play a (recorded) piece of music or a soundscape, preferably one that is unknown to the group, is three minutes or less in duration, and is not a song with text. Ask everyone to simply listen. Play it again and ask everyone to map out the general form without using Western notation. Ask: how can you represent (notate) sonic details in time? Sometimes I will bring colored pencils, crayons, and blank paper. For a playful version, bring a long roll of butcher paper for a collaborative exercise.

6
DESSERT

There are two choices for dessert: "Listen, as a Bird in Flight" and "Recipe for Mixing."

"Listen, as a Bird in Flight" is a small, sweet text piece to nibble with a group. It is inspired by Pauline Oliveros's *Sonic Meditations* (1974). To see the full context for incorporating this work for music-nature explorations, see Hahn (2017a).

Listen, as a Bird in Flight

Form two groups.
Group 1.
    Sits or lies down
    creating earth chatter . . .
    sounds of trees, trucks, insects,
    parades, footsteps, and so on.
Group 2.
    Walks around the space at
    different speeds
    periodically sounding moving air
    and winds.
    Continue, listen and remember.

Recipe for Mixing

for Kimiko

"Recipe for Mixing" was originally published in *Other Tongues: Mixed-Raced Women Speak Out* (Hahn 2010).

Every fall, tendrils creep out of my mulch pile, out of my half-eaten debris, carted out religiously after the kitchen scrap bucket holds no more. What climbing plants could these be, wandering from the muck, reaching to warm sunlight?

To my delight, the first year these mystery plants bore fruit—pumpkins and carnival squash.

The second year, similar leaves and vines crawled along the rich soil, grasping at any stable staff to hoist skyward. The trailing green vines—now bearing pumpkins with speckles, squash, and ornamental gourds—seemed to intertwine sensuously. Caressing gently here. Climbing and interweaving almost competitively there. Prickly broad leaves forming shade, camouflaging fruit below.
What's to hide?

Year three, delicate tendrils return.
I watch eagerly as each vine sprawls out with whimsical, yet slow dance steps.
Later, after the performance, they recline longingly.
What secret appears under shaded leaves?
Radiant orange hybrids of gourds, squash, pumpkin—striped and speckled pumpkins, carnival squash with gourd knobs, and long gourds wearing stems befitting jack-o-lanterns. Three years of fertile cross-pollination, as one anther's pollen mingled with the other. None can simply pass for pumpkin, nor squash, nor gourd any longer. The labor from mulch bore no Latin-named offspring. Each vine offers unique offspring with no sense of belonging, except with those traveling along the vine.

7
RESOURCES

This chapter provides a brief explanation of freewriting and examples of works by workshop participants inspired by sensory prompts.

Freewriting

I employ the word "freewriting" throughout this book largely because the practice has become common in most classrooms. However, it is important to briefly clarify the background and process for the current context.

The origin of freewriting practices that aim to free up one's critical, self-conscious writing is a bit blurred. Connections have been made to Freud and "tapping the unconscious." The Surrealists and Dadaists had a writing process called "automatic writing" aiming to draw from the unconscious or, in some contexts, a mystical or spiritual realm. Readers may find Abi Curtis's perspective, challenging the notion of tapping "the unconscious," interesting (2009). Dorothea Brande's foundational book *Becoming a Writer* ([1934] 2019) encouraged writers to harness the unconscious through writing and to "write anything that comes to your head" (31) as a means of freeing up one's personal obstacles and what is considered right or wrong during the writing process. Brande proposed a regular writing practice, preferably done early in the day when everyday matters have not populated one's thoughts. Decades later, the practice of "freewriting" caught on wildly due to the efforts of Peter Elbow, among others. Freewriting is, by design, interdisciplinary, as it does not require specialized training or expert knowledge about writing instruction. After the 1970s it became common for writers' workshops, grade schools, and colleges to incorporate time for continuous writing in the classroom as a prewriting technique. The practice of freewriting continues to be used in many pedagogical settings. Elbow wrote, "Freewriting is the easiest way to get words on paper and the best all-around practice in writing that I know. To do a freewriting exercise, simply force yourself to write without stopping for ten minutes. Sometimes you will produce good writing, but that's not the point" ([1981] 1998, 13). If you are interested in details of his writing techniques, I strongly recommend reading Elbow's texts on writing pedagogy; there are many, but to start see *Writing without Teachers* ([1973] 1998) and *Writing with Power* ([1981] 1998). Other, more recent, recommendations for establishing a regular writing practice to generate material are Natalie Goldberg's *Writing Down the Bones: Freeing the Writer Within* ([1986] 2016) and *Wild Mind: Living the Writer's Life* (1990) and James Pennebaker and John Evans's *Expressive Writing: Words That Heal* (2014). A book focusing on the principles of writing practice, Linda Adler-Kassner and Elizabeth Wardle's edited book *Naming What we Know: Threshold Concepts of Writing Studies* (2015), might also be helpful to frame writing as one of many ways of expressing one's self.

For my purposes in this book, leaders only need to know the basics of the freewriting approach and consider how to adjust the description for their setting and voice. During the first meeting of a workshop or class I briefly explain what the freewriting process is. I say something along the lines of this:

> Please take out your sketchbooks and writing implement and have them close by. Each meeting we will start with a sensory prompt. During the prompt please allow yourself to immerse yourself in the experience. Directly after the prompt, please do not talk. Open your notebooks and "freewrite" for the next ten to fifteen minutes.
>
> "Freewrite" refers to a generative process of writing where everyone writes continuously for a designated period of time. It does not need to make sense or be grammatically correct. No one will be reading your freewriting. What is important is that you are writing as fluidly as possible. Try writing with an uninhibited flow, "without thought," or extemporaneously. I propose that it is a kind of writing (or drawing) that directly stems from your sensory,

bodily experience. Most importantly: don't stop writing. The point is to fluidly generate as much text as possible.

It's important that the description of freewriting is offered *prior* to the sensory prompt and that it is brief so that it does not interrupt the sensing-to-expressing flow. I find it is valuable to repeat a shorter version of the description for the next few meetups, often while the participants are opening their notebooks. But, as in all of the recipes in this book, find your own voice and make the workshops your own. Feel free to "try on" my voice for size, but then allow the practice to form to your personality and context.

Work Prompted by "Shifting Point of View" Recipe

The prompt: Consider someone's or something's perspective or point of view. For the example piece below, the class was prompted to write from the perspective of someone or something small and/or big.

"The Size of Your Misconceptions" by Edlyn Terrazas (published with permission of author)

They see us as "small." Not in stature, but in "status." Easily crushed by a looming shiny leather brown shoe that descends without forgiveness. "Small" is a derogatory term to *them*. It is something weak that can be manipulated. And *they* see themselves as "BIG"—strong, powerful, and dictating the future. We are "small" because our roads are made out of dirt, because our roofs were assembled out of fronds from the plants we nurture, because our means of transportation are our capable limbs, and because currency does not flow through our veins. *They* are "BIG" because *they* have money. *They* are strong because *they* prey on the "small." Perhaps, when both of our roads were not concrete, when both of us did not have running water at our disposal at all time, when we knew 75% of our community, then maybe, there were no labels. No "small" nor "BIG." However, when *they* acquired a force they wielded to use in their favor and against us, *they* began to take. And take. And that is when *they* saw *they* were making us "small." They liked it. *We BIGs liked it.*

According to *them,* I am "small." My family is "small." Our neighbors are "small" as well. "Smalls" all around make a community. Here, our fellow "smalls" support the actions of other "smalls." When Dona Lucia is unable to go to *el abarrote* because the rain has created a muddy barrier where her frail legs can easily be ensnared in, I take off my worn sandals, trudge through the mud lifting it with me and causing it to strike my back, and pay 10 *pesos* for the *chile* she needs to prepare food. *How sentimental. Dona Lucia is still making children do her bidding.* And later that day she invites me to eat with her *nietos*. Two "smalls" working together. They are not forced to. They do it for their community. We lend a helping hand; an alien ideology to the "BIGS." *We help when it is convenient. When I can get something out of it.* We are not the "weak" *they* associate with the status of "small," for if we were so weak the "BIGS" would not seek our labors that give them their "BIG" status. *We use you.* In their eyes we are under their rule, their control. We are the citizens to their dynasty. *It is our world. We let you merely participate.*

And sadly, sometimes us "smalls" believe it. *Because it is factual.* As the seasonal yellow bus comes for us at 4 A.M. when the sun has not yet broken the darkness's curtains, the "BIGS" really do look big. The bus jostles us awake in the opposite direction of where the sun is making its big entrance, and we are taken to more dirt, rows upon rows with green mohawks bursting from it. We work the fields. *I remember.* The "BIG's" field. *You work for us, not with us.* For even though currency is not pumped by our hearts, it is still necessary to sustain the "smalls." *It is the only thing that gets anyone anywhere.* And it is at times supplied by the "BIGS" through working the land. Hunched down, with our hands outstretched, our already dirty fingers pierce the dirt searching for the potatoes that will fill our bags. Pick it up, put it in the bag. Shift the dirt, pick the potato up, put it in the bag. *Until the satchels are full, and then you get another one to fill up after it. And another. Until we say so.* The sun beats on our necks, ruling the bandanas tied around them useless. *I was not going back there.* As I look around, I notice that we all do the same mechanical movements, returning back to the land. The land: dirt. Dirt: our roads, it still comes back to us. *I did not want the dirt, I wanted advancement. No matter what.* And the spell is broken. *The spell never broke for me.* It is not long before we come back to our senses. The land is part of us, not *theirs*. Us "weaklings" are what give the "BIGS" the impression of being strong, because that is what the "smalls" embody: strength. *They see strength, we see the truth: helplessness and foolish hope.*

They can continue to characterize me as "small" and I can grow into the best "small" thing ever because small fits anywhere. *You fit where we want you to fit.* Me and my fellow "smalls" can do anything because our attitudes allow us to mold and fit anywhere. *Attitudes will get them nowhere.* From our "small" perspective we can see the "BIGs" and their behaviors. We will shy away from their ignorance and façade of strength, for nobody that is strong should oppress others, even if they think others are "small." *Then they will shy away from triumph.* I wish to become a better "small," not a "BIG." *Not possible. I once wished that too.* I wish to rise up, but not leave others behind, to remember my *pueblo,* and do what the "BIGs" neglected: to return to my fellow "smalls" and help them reach their goals and inspire others to do so. *I tried.* "Smalls" continuing to support each other. *But I could not, I failed.* Adding to each other, until *they* see our true nature of fortitude. As we rise, *they* will try to knock us down, but the "BIGs" cannot because we are powerful, successful, and invincible. In that moment *they* will be aware of their misconception of "SMALL." *I hope so.*

They see us as "BIG." We see ourselves as triumphant. *They* view us as "BIG" because we did not stop once we reached success. We desired more, and we went to seize it. *At what cost?* It is not our fault *they* are "small." *They* are "small" because *they* chose to stay in *el pueblo* they say they hold so dear. *Our pueblo is not the issue. They* are "small" because it is easier to victimize themselves than to accept defeat. *It was not us who commenced the "*BIG*" and "small" division.* Perhaps, when we all had the chance to improve ourselves, both "BIGs" and "smalls" would have advanced in life and no one would be whining. *Your improvement came by leeching off of us.* We are affluent and prosperous. If that is "BIG" to the "smalls," then yes, yes, we are "BIG" at any cost.

Spanish Text Translation

Abarrote—store
Chile—peppers
Nietos—grandchildren
Pesos—Mexican currency
Pueblo—town

Work Prompted by "Bonding in Parallel" Recipe

"Excavating Time" by Lorelei Wagner and Tomie Hahn (published with permission of authors)

A dumping ground full of
possibilities.
Piles of
"Huh?"
"Ooooooo!!!"
"What IS that?!"
"This is where that has been!?"
"I FOUND IT!!"
Surrounded by scattered, tattered,
half-baked, raw ingredients that
coalesce into a giant mass of swirls,
loops, humps, dots, curves, lines
of all colors, shapes, weights, sizes,
densities.
Occasionally flags protrude rudely
signaling to the Seeker that

This Is Something Important

Excavating this terrain can be complicated, deceiving, frustrating.
But most of the adventures create
excitement, inspiration, motivation,
energy

From dusting off pieces that have
been buried under the weight of the
Fresh and new.

Despite their age and slight
Decomposition,
They are able to be restored,
renewed, reimagined
So long as their original form hasn't
been altered by some outside force:
Stains
Tears
A little one's curiosity.

Worn and tarnished to
The point of not
reflecting
yet,

the grey takes on a shape
of time
small dots appear
the tarnish even offers
relief
curiously at the edge of beauty
the shapes of clouds or

shapes of . . . is it
grapes?
stalks?
imagined curves.

the oval!
Perfect for scooping
and the pleasures of taste
every
morsel
to dissolve and nourish.

Where did you come from?
There in the heap of saved
objects in time
saved to tarnish over time

saved for a special day in the future?
or an occasion that never arose
simply because
simply because . . .
life was never lived like that or
these were forgotten

over time

(The left column was inspired by journal notebooks and the right column by antique dessert spoons.)

Work Prompted by "Scent of Time" Recipe

"Lemon Memories" (excerpt) by Abdullah Alshehri (by permission of author)

A strong scent of lemon took me thousands of miles away, 6500 miles to be exact, back to my home in Saudi Arabia. That bright scent sparked a memory in my past. It reminded me of the times my mother and I spent together to make a famous local dish called stuffed grape leaves and how I became better at making them.

Stuffed grape leaves, also known as dolma, are the fresh leaves picked from the grapevine plant and stuffed with a mixture of rice, spices, and sometimes meat. They can be served warm or cold on a plate with slices of lemon, hence the sour taste and the sharp smell. In Saudi Arabia, stuffed grape leaves are a ubiquitous appetizer that is found almost everywhere.

I have liked eating stuffed grape leaves ever since I was a kid, and so did my mother. However, my mother preferred making them at home using her own mixture and ingredients. When I was eleven years old, I asked my mother to teach me how to make stuffed grape leaves because I wanted to make them by myself. Every time I came home from school on Tuesdays, my mother and I would sit at the dining table and make stuffed grape leaves. On the first Tuesday, my mother told me to watch her make it all by herself. She prepared the ingredients, put them on the leaves, and then folded them while I cut some lemon slices. The hard part of making them was folding and rolling the leaves while keeping the mixture inside of them, and I paid full attention while my mother was doing this part.

Two weeks later, on the third Tuesday, I started to fold the grape leaves with my mother. It was not easy at the beginning, but I got better week by week as I imitated my mother's technique of folding. "Grape leaves taste good, but they take forever to make," my mother used to say. After making them by my own hands and feeling tired, I understood what she meant by that. Making grape leaves was very exhausting for just an appetizer dish.

Overall, my mother and I collaborated and harmonized well as a team when making stuffed grape leaves. First, she would take care of cooking the ingredients while I cut some lemon slices. Cutting lemon slices has been my role since I started learning how to cook stuffed grape leaves; thus, the lemon scent always reminds me of this story. Then, she would pass me the cooked mixture so that I would place it on the leaves. Lastly, using her technique, I would roll and fold the leaves making sure to keep the mixture inside.

Learning how to make stuffed grape leaves with my mother is one of the most meaningful memories that I value and appreciate greatly. It taught me consistency and how to be persistent while learning something in life. Most importantly, writing about this story made me realize that some small and simple memories might seem commonplace to some people. However, these memories can be of great value.

"Now!" Recipe Responses

Below are several responses I received for the recipe "Now!" The time stamps represent the time I received participants' email or text. For our seminar I printed the responses without names so that our discussions focused on the sensory experience and responses.

Now! listen (sound prompt)

3:31 P.M.
library computer room, the shuffling papers, typing becoming heavier and faster and at times light depending on the size and weight of the keys. boots on a carpeted floor, perhaps meant to stifle the sound but it only amplifies the thud of the heel. nostril breathing, heavy but controlled. squeaking of an opening door down the hall. heavy slam. light beat boxing and the zipping up of a backpack

3:34 P.M.
Keys jingling, the hum of appliances in other rooms. Breathy air being pushed out of a neglected humidifier. Doors opening, closing. Stagnancy. My hair brushing against my body as I search for noises with my eyes.

3:50 P.M.
Creaking doors
A man talking loudly in an Asian language; Chinese? Korean? . . .
A girl, a bit farther away than the man, speaking in English
It's hard not to listen to this since I understand, even though it's not as loud. If I listen to her, I don't listen to any other sounds, let alone another conversation that I don't understand.
Other people, farther still, speaking in mumbles

A cough in front of me
A sniffle behind
Ringing in my ears from my headache
My phone buzzes. It's very hard not to open my eyes now.
The doors cracking closed.
A blinker clicking.

5:22 P.M.
Clicking (computer mouses)
quiet whispering
approaching footsteps
crumbling of a potato chip bag (which made me hungry!)
constant stream of quiet noise (I'm guessing it was coming from the air conditioner or heater)
body movement
calmness
my mind felt more "open" as I listened

7:30 P.M.
I feel lucky that when it rains, I can fool myself that cars cruising slowly past my window sound like crashing, rolling waves. I can yearn for the West Coast, specifically, for some reason, the peace of Santa Barbara, in that fleeting second of tangible likeness. The heavy silences punctuated by cars makes me realize the sound of this place is lonely. The buzz of a city, even a place spread as far out as Los Angeles, feels like a humming hive that creates the illusion of autonomy and purpose, while these creaky quiet woods challenge the mind with silence. The constant whisper of my tower fan, even in the winter, seems like a feeble attempt on my part to comfort my mind with sound pollution.

7:56 P.M.
Air circulating (humming), typing on keyboards and mouse clicking, a car driving by around the bend in the rain, light rain (faintly), distant footsteps from the floor above, a car driving in the opposite direction, buttons clicking on a cell phone, a door opening, followed by feet scuffing on a door mat, followed by footsteps becoming fainter as a person walks away.

Works Prompted by "Through the Portal" Recipe

"17 Years as a Beat Cop" by Michael Schrider (published with permission of author)

Seventeen years as a beat cop, 18 years patrolling this side of town, stopping petty thefts, responding to robberies and the occasional gunshots. Seventeen years and it was all about to end, this was my last patrol before being promoted to chief. So of course, tonight was the night that I am chasing down this deranged soul who just stabbed that poor clerk.

These were the words that plodded along to the pounding of the soles of my boots against the concrete as I flew after the perp. My partner and I had been making our routine rounds when we heard a scream across the street. We rushed over to see what the deal was and saw a man burst through the door of a nearby corner store. He had a ski mask covering his face, had a bag barely zipped full over his shoulder, and had a knife, bloody to the handle, in his hand. My partner and I shared a brief glance, then started running. He peeled off into the store to see if he could do anything to help and I tore off after the man. The perp bowled people over and toppled trash cans, horns were blaring as he ran across roads, dogs barked as he flew past them; it was a deafening cacophony of sounds as he tried to evade me. I heard none of it.

He tripped, stumbling over a poorly laid sidewalk tile. I was right on his heels. I lunged, plowing into him, carrying us both careening through the storefront window. A thunderous crash accompanied the explosion of pain as my shoulder and face shattered the hard glass. I heard the soft tinkling of delicate shards peppering the ground around us as our bodies hit the ground.

Blearily opening my eyes, I looked around. I rolled over and tried to stand up, bracing myself on my hands and pushing. Hearing a crunching sound and feeling a sharp pain in my hand as I pressed it down, I grimaced. Cursing under my breath, I looked at my palms. I muttered angrily and brushed my hands against my pants. I must have fallen asleep while watching T.V. again and spilled Doritos all over the couch and ground. Wearily I trudged to the closet, opened the door and grabbed the broom and dustpan. I turned and squinted in irritation. Why did my shoulder hurt? I hadn't left the house in two days, much less done anything strenuous enough to hurt myself. I must have just slept on it wrong.

My mess cleaned up, I put the broom back in the closet then sat back on the couch to see what new tragedy was plaguing the world today. I flipped through the news stations, looking for anything even remotely interesting. I flipped to channel 17 and the remote control started to act up, I banged it on the couch a few times to no avail. It was a droll, yet somewhat sad, story about a beat cop who was stabbed during a foot chase. They showed a picture of a shattered window, broken glass, and a fresh bloodstain on the ground. Finally, the little light on the remote control flashed on and I kept flipping through channels. My favorite show flashed over the screen and all thoughts of the news and outside world were gone from my mind.

"Beyond Realism" by Amelia Farquharson (published with permission of author)

I delicately picked up my set of pencils, briefly deciding which one to use. I selected my lightest pencil, so I could create a rough sketch of my idea before committing to the design. Carrying my choice of writing instruments across the room, my feet sank into the plush carpet. I spun my desk chair around and sat down facing my polished wood desk. After getting comfortable in the chair, I turned on my lamp to brighten my workspace, and let my hand start gliding over the pad of paper.

Starting with some long curves extending intermittently between the top and bottom edges of my drawing, I slowly started to sketch horizontal lines crossing the bottom half of the paper, intersecting some of the rough curves. I then drew a floating, egg-like shape in the center of the image and managed to rough out some lines beneath it to resemble shoulders, then arms, then a torso, and finally legs. My pencil maneuvered around the figure, drawing thin, dancing lines in the air, which I would return to at a later time. I sat back from my light sketch, and I admired the quick yet concise idea I had put on paper. Time for details.

I switched immediately to my darkest pencil and took the vertical curves, beginning to block out their trunks and give them branches. The cylindrical trunks gained a new sense of life with each movement of my hand; the bark seemed to grow right out of the paper, and I could practically feel the trees under my hand as I finished fleshing out the last set of roots on a large oak in the corner of the paper.

The bases of these trees now connected to a firmer ground, with grass lines dotting the horizontals I had created earlier. I spent time detailing each inch of the ground, my pencil giving the ground new life with the addition of the grass. Each blade looked frozen in motion, a solid sea of thin lines waving across the paper. Amidst the scene I created, the skeleton of a person I had drawn out now gained a more specific shape, with muscles defining the formerly twig-like limbs and body. They stood amongst the trees and grass, and the dancing lines surrounding them became leaves, swirling around in a ballad on the wind. I watched as a leaf sailed from a branch to brush my cheek. The leaf tickled as it kissed my skin, then continued around my head before drifting slowly to the ground along with the others. I could hear the crunch of freshly shed leaves as I shifted between my feet and enjoyed the crisp autumn weather.

Now I needed color. I stretched my arms and hands after hunching over the drawing for the better part of an hour and pulled out my watercolors. I selected a shade of light brown and started on the bark of the trees. The trunks were a beautiful hue around this time of year, the color of their bark making the leaves seem all the more vivid. I walked over to a tree, and put my hand on the beige wood, feeling the wrinkles of the tree's skin. I looked down at the ground, and the bright green grass smiled back up at me between the carpet of fallen leaves, which now glowed with a spectrum of colors.

I looked up at the canopy of this simple, little forest, and felt the warm sun on my face. I raised my hand to shield my eyes from the light and to get a better look at my surroundings. The light twinkled between shifting branches and foliage. Amidst the leaves, I caught a glimpse of a deep blue sky. I noticed the beams of sunlight sprinkling down from beyond the trees and admired how they highlighted the forest. Brown trunks, decorated with speckles of golden, orange leaves, glowed a vibrant amber, and blades of grass twinkled like emeralds.

Pulling my cyan scarf around my neck to fend off the gentle nip of the autumn wind, I caught another falling leaf to examine it. I ran my hands over the surface of the leaf, feeling its small veins, and admired the colors I had given it. The base of the leaf was a lime green, gradating to scarlet at its tips. I placed the beautiful leaf into my pocket, hoping I wouldn't crush it. I then swiveled in my chair and stood up. The fibers of my carpet felt soft between my toes and I sighed in satisfaction. After another hour of coloring in the image, I didn't know where to go with it next. Running my finger over the picture, I traced the lines with my nail. The colors were all in place, I stood comfortably in my scarf, sweater and jeans, and the leaves now vividly circled the air. I packed away my watercolors and put my pencil set cozily back in its box, and then in the wooden desk drawer. I looked one more time at my autumn scene, and picked up the thick, watercolor paper in my tired hands. It almost felt fragile, like I could tear it up any second if my hand twitched. I decided to set the leaf back on the ground before I crumbled nature's beautiful artwork, and I walked away into the vermilion and sage colored forest.

Work Prompted by "Wearables" Recipe

"On Being an Eternal Scout" by Katherine Tyrol (published with permission of author), excerpt from her final paper for the graduate seminar Between Art and Anthropology

PAX EAST, GEEKERY, AND UNIFORMITY

I love geeks. I mean, first I loved geekdom. My mom passed on her love of Superman to me, and my dad introduced me to Star Trek when I was seven and the first episode of "The Next Generation" premiered. Both of my parents encouraged intellectual pursuits above all others and also the idea that intelligence is the best tool to solve a problem (a trait I would say is at the root of geekdom). And then my first friends were geeks—the most advanced math students in second grade, all four of us a little bit socially awkward and delighted by knowledge and problem-solving and—us girls following the boys' lead here—the movie "Ghostbusters" which got re-enacted during recess on a fairly regular basis. There was never a time that being smart and obsessive and detail-oriented and at least a little bit outcast weren't central tenets of my life. I have never loved someone who wasn't largely living in their head.

Expanding outward from my parents' interests, I found more geek stories that spoke to me about the imaginary worlds on which I can project our own complicated and difficult world—The X-Files and Firefly and Doctor Who, numerous science fiction authors (chief among them Ursula K. Le Guin and Janet Kagan and Amy Thomson), iconic video games like "The Legend of Zelda" and "World of Warcraft" and "Portal" and, most recently, the brilliant podcast "Welcome to Night Vale" which plays delightfully with notions of reality and community and propriety. My interest in these things has brought me great personal comfort and joy and also forged or reinforced many of the bonds with others that I still have in my life.

But geeks hurt me—on a grand and a tiny scale—all the time. They omit women from their language and their stories and their activities and their workplaces in all but the most decorative of positions. They blithely stomp on your heart because they forget that hearts are used for anything, and they ignore the plight of others for having been trapped inside their own head and so their own experience for too long.

Geeks as a group occupy this tenuous space shaped by the tension between the strictures of a highly normative life—middle or upper-middle class incomes, jobs that rely on industry and firmly imposed order on human processes, the prestige that comes with working in high tech in 21st century America—and a number of underlying principles that drive them to deviance, such as a strong belief in independence stemming from having come of age while largely ostracized and an enthusiastic do-it-yourself/hacker aesthetic that promotes anti-corporate and even anti-legal-system values.

This means that collectively, geeks frequently disregard concerns about social justice, a cause that I see as foundational to successful analysis of the world, of individuals, of social interactions. Which brings me to Penny Arcade and PAX East. PAX East (Penny Arcade Expo) is a gaming convention held annually in Boston and which I've attended for the last three years. It's organized by the creators of the webcomic "Penny Arcade" who wanted a venue for their fans to meet up and play games together. I've been very happy at this convention—I've felt safe and welcomed; unlike other cons I've seen no hint of shame either towards women (with the classic dismissal of "fake geek girl") or to "newbs" (newcomers, who are often unwelcome at games or other geek events for their lack of skill or technical or cultural knowledge—frequently interchangeable in geek culture).

THE PLAN

In my two years so far in graduate school, my research interests have solidified around the body, cultural sameness, representation, and how identity intersects with all those things. I found my personal interests turning more towards my body—how to be more present in it and what it means to me and the world—and particularly towards cosplay.

I hypothesized that there was a way I could address all of these things in a mini-ethnographic and artistic project—my passion for geeks and the stories created by and for them, my fears and disappointments in the geek community, my struggles around body, identity, Scouting and community—with my ambition to begin cosplaying myself and specifically a segment of "Welcome to Night Vale" that described their vision of Scouting called Eternal Scouts.

So, I learned to embroider by reading and practicing through the shortest days of the year. I studied Boy Scout badges loaned to me from a friend to supplement distant memories of my own. And finally, I designed and embroidered six merit badges meant to synthesize the ideas I was working with: citizenship, health and bodies, conformity, and surveillance. I attached five pieces of troop regalia and these six badges to a sash I had sewn. Worn on top of a hand-me-down polo shirt from my grandmother and a dress I had designed based on my Brownie Girl Scout uniform, I had an Eternal Scout costume.

THE CON

PAX East has about 25,000 attendees spread out over a 500,000 square foot expo floor (which showcases maybe half again or double that when you include surrounding theaters, lobbies, and corridors). Numerous tracks of panels, workshops, and entertainment are scheduled for the entire fourteen-hour day followed by offsite after-parties. Video games of all sorts—modern and antique; arcade machines, PC, and consoles (such as the Nintendo Wii and the Xbox); for the use of tiny or large groups or for individuals—are available throughout the con. Hundreds of board and card games are available through a lending library and tournaments or lessons for dozens of games are ongoing. The crowds are huge and in the most dense areas, chaotic. Finding or coordinating with your friends, teammates, or traveling companions is always time-consuming and confusing given the crowd, the noise level, routine losses of cell or text service, and remote hotels and restaurants. It is a messy, exciting, delightful time, but it is also tiring. I end up having to expend a great deal of energy to cope with the crowds, the extensive walking, and the disorganization. An important reason to consider this is that my every observation and interaction was influenced by the compromised state this perpetual energy deficit produced.

The con is full of cosplay. My favorite cosplays are the most elaborately adorned women alien dresses and medieval gowns and bizarre reimagined spacesuits. I also particularly enjoy people dressed as inanimate objects, anyone dressed as something or someone from the Doctor Who universe, and any highly detailed costume or body paint. I was especially struck this year by how many plus-sized women I saw cosplaying and often in revealing outfits, something I don't remember seeing at all at previous cons I've attended. The most memorable such costume was a woman dressed very convincingly—in a vibrant red wig, green stockings, and a mesh minidress covered in vines—as the Batman villain Poison Ivy.

THE COSPLAY

Saturday was the day I'd selected for my cosplay, since it's the most popular day of the con and so, presumably, will have the most attendees. That morning, I woke up cheerfully bright and early in the morning. In the bathroom at the friend's condo where I was staying, I dressed slowly and carefully, savoring the moment of the whole costume finally coming together. I wore some undergarments I don't normally to try to smooth out the shape of my body to maximize the smooth, almost mechanistic look the military and so scouts aspire to in donning uniform. I donned my sash, my favorite part of the costume, last and almost immediately took a selfie in the bathroom mirror to share on Facebook with folks back home who had been following along with the crafting process, excited about my impending cosplay.

As I walked from my friend's condo to my car, I was hard-pressed not to giggle to myself at how strange and unbelievable it felt to actually be in this creation I had envisioned and out in broad daylight looking likely quite odd for an adult woman. I removed my sash for my stop at Starbucks, but even so, by the time I arrived at the con, I already felt quite ordinary in my uniform. Indeed, I felt so ordinary, that it came as no surprise in the moment, that the other con-goers did not comment or even look differently at me.

I spent most of the daytime walking around the convention center. There was an ongoing game to try to scan all of the QR codes hidden throughout the center, so it seemed a good time to search for them as I visited different areas of the con to see how I felt in costume in different environments. I was disheartened to learn that, in this world of exotic, outlandish, and alien costuming, I felt very ordinary. This was reflected in my fellow attendees, only one of whom outside my social circle commented on my appearance in the entire course of the day. I found myself fantasizing about ways I could revise the costume to garner more attention and was disappointed that my mind went almost immediately to ways to sexualize my costume. With the exception of performing an altogether different and more iconic cosplay, I found that no matter how I played around with the design, I could not think of a way to emulate the cosplayers that were getting attention that did not involve more skin, more cleavage, more titillation and much less cloth. I don't share this story about my thought process to criticize or malign the cosplayers who do so; there are more revealing cosplays I fully intend to attempt someday, but given the things I want to do with this costume—talk about identity and how it is created and can be broken, point out the ironies in our definitions of good citizenship, question what is and isn't ordinary—it would be cheating as far as I'm concerned to sexualize myself or my character for attention entirely separate for those ideas. It is the cosplay equivalent of offering free pizza to get people to attend your lecture.

There were some triumphs, my delight at bringing a vision I cared so much about to fruition chief among them. Additionally, my friends that I saw that day were very excited about the costume—cheering when we finally met up late in the day, photographing me and discussing various aspects of costume design. And there is another reason that I think this lack of reception is a success: I am freed now to be far more outlandish the next time I cosplay.

8

CORDIAL CLOSURE

Imagine how every choice we make resonates or reverberates into the world. How might our sensory awareness of the time and space we inhabit affect our choices? What are the sources of our sensory impulses and responses? My hope is that these recipes offer in-the-moment sensory encounters to spark creativity and insights, helping us to situate our personal responses to these questions.

What I have learned as an explorer of sense is that our personal sensory awareness illustrates who we are at that particular moment. How various modalities of sense express (manifest) energy and existence over time warrants noticing. In turn, we can express (convey) what we notice. What we experience and how we choose to express what we have encountered render a unique landscape of self. These landscapes mirror the wondrous complexity of sensory practices we embody over time.

There are many approaches for incorporating sensibilities in our expressive lives, such as in writing, performing, and art making. In some contexts, sensory rich, "thick descriptions" in writing/making provide readers/witnesses with lush, sensuous details of our experience and imagination. In other contexts, minimizing specifics and offering only a bare suggestion of a scene allows the receivers of our work to imaginatively fill in the details. For myself—perhaps because I am fascinated with modes of transmission and the senses—the form and what I desire to convey intertwine so deeply that I cannot untangle the mesh. One experience affords several vivid articulations, or expressions, to "make sense" of the surreal realm that I inhabit.

References

Adler-Kassner, Linda, and Elizabeth Wardle, eds. 2015. *Naming What We Know: Threshold Concepts of Writing Studies*. Boulder: University Press of Colorado.

Ahmed, Sara. 2012. *On Being Included: Racism and Diversity in Institutional Life*. Durham, NC: Duke University Press.

Barbezat, Daniel, and Mirabai Bush. 2014. *Contemplative Practices in Higher Education: Powerful Methods to Transform Teaching and Learning*. San Francisco: Jossey-Bass.

Barrett, Estelle, and Barbara Bolt, eds. 2007. *Practice as Research: Approaches to Creative Arts Enquiry*. London: I. B. Tauris.

Bednarik, Robert. 2016. "Rock Art and Pareidolia." *Rock Art Research* 33, no. 2: 167–81.

Behar, Ruth. 1996. *The Vulnerable Observer: Anthropology That Breaks Your Heart*. Boston: Beacon Press.

Bell, Catherine. (1992) 2009. *Ritual Theory, Ritual Practice*. Oxford: Oxford University Press.

———. 2009. *Ritual: Perspectives and Dimensions*. Oxford: Oxford University Press.

Bhattacharya, Kakali. 2017. *Fundamentals of Qualitative Research: A Practical Guide*. New York: Routledge.

Brande, Dorothea. (1934) 2019. *Becoming a Writer*. New Delhi: General Press.

Chabris, Christopher, and Daniel Simons. 2010. *The Invisible Gorilla: How Our Intuitions Deceive Us*. New York: Crown, Random House.

Classen, Constance. 1993. *Worlds of Sense: Exploring the Senses across Cultures*. New York: Routledge.

Curtis, Abi. 2009. "Rethinking the Unconscious in Creative Writing Pedagogy." *New Writing: The International Journal for the Practice and Theory of Creative Writing* 6, no. 2: 105–16.

DeVale, Sue Carole. 1990. "Organizing Organology." *Selected Reports in Ethnomusicology* 8, no. 1: 34.

Elbow, Peter. (1973) 1998. *Writing without Teachers*. New York: Oxford University Press.

———. (1981) 1998. *Writing with Power: Techniques for Mastering the Writing Process*. New York: Oxford University Press.

Elliot, Denielle, and Dara Culhane, eds. 2017. *A Different Kind of Ethnography: Imaginative Practices and Creative Methodologies*. Toronto: University of Toronto Press.

Ergas, Oren. 2017. *Reconstructing "Education" through Mindful Attention: Positioning the Mind at the Center of Curriculum and Pedagogy*. London: Palgrave Macmillan.

Ericsson, Anders, and Robert Pool. 2017. *Peak: Secrets from the New Science of Expertise*. Boston: Eamon Dolan/Mariner Books.

Freire, Paulo. 2007. *Pedagogy of the Oppressed*. New York: Continuum.

Friedman, Ken, Owen Smith, and Lauren Sawchyn, eds. 2002. *The Fluxus Performance Workbook*. Performance Research e-publication.

Gershon, Walter. 2011. "Introduction towards a Sensual Curriculum." *Journal of Curriculum Theorizing* 27, no. 2: 1–16.

Goldberg, Natalie. (1986) 2016. *Writing Down the Bones: Freeing the Writer Within*. Boulder: Shambhala Publications.

———. 1990. *Wild Mind: Living the Writer's Life*. New York: Bantam.

Hahn, Tomie. 2006. "Emerging Voices—Encounters with Reflexivity." In "Women, Arts, Politics/Power." Special issue, *Atlantis: A Women's Studies Journal / Revue d'etudes sur les femmes* 30, no. 2: 88–99.

———. 2007. *Sensational Knowledge: Embodying Culture through Japanese Dance*. Middletown, CT: Wesleyan University Press.

———. 2010. "Recipe for Mixing." In *Other Tongues: Mixed-Race Women Speak Out*, edited by A. DeRango-Adem and A. Thompson, 251. Toronto: Inanna Press.

———. 2015. "One Eyebrow Raised: A Recipe for Sound and Movement." *Women in Music: A Journal of Gender and Culture* (special issue devoted to the work of Suzanne Cusick) 19:15–17.

———. 2017a. "Layered Listenings: Lessons of the Land, Air and Sea." In "Teaching Ecomusicology." Special issue, *Journal of Music History Pedagogy* 8, no. 1: 86–90.

———. 2017b. "Performing Ethnography Out of Bounds: An Essay on Transmission Failure." In *Out of Bounds: Ethnography, Music, and History*, edited by I. Monson, C. Oja, and R. Wolf, 19–29. Cambridge, MA: Harvard University Press.

Hahn, Tomie, and Curtis Bahn. 2002. "*Pikapika*—The Collaborative Composition of an Interactive Sonic Character." *Organised Sound: An International Journal of Music Technology* 7, no. 3: 229–38.

———. 2004. *Pikapika* (interactive live-electronic dance) in *Recording Field, H.* DVD. Kingston: Deep Listening Publications.

Hahn, Tomie, Louise Campbell, Lindsay Vogt, Simon Rose, George Blake, Catherine Lee, Sherrie Tucker, François Mouillot, Jovanna Milović, and Pete

Williams. 2016. "Banding Encounters—Embodied Practices in Improvisation." In *Negotiated Moments: Improvisation, Sound and Subjectivity*, edited by G. Siddall and E. Waterman, 149–67. Durham, NC: Duke University Press.

Hahn, Tomie, and J. Scott Jordan. 2014. "Anticipation and Embodied Knowledge: Observations of Enculturating Bodies." *Journal of Cognitive Education and Psychology* (special issue) 13, no. 2: 272–84.

———. 2017. "Sensible Objects: Intercorporeality and Enactive Knowing through Things." In *Intercorporeality: Beyond the Body*, edited by C. Meyer, J. Streeck, and J. S. Jordon. 267–87. Oxford: Oxford University Press.

Heller, Monica. 1988. *Codeswitching: Anthropological Sociolinguistic Perspectives*. Berlin: Mouton de Gruyter.

Heywood, Ian. 2017. *Sensory Arts and Design*. London: Bloomsbury Academic.

hooks, bell. 1994. *Teaching to Transgress: Teaching as a Practice of Freedom*. New York: Routledge.

Horowitz, Alexandra. 2016. *Being a Dog: Following the Dog into a World of Smell*. New York: Scribner.

———. 2017. "Learn to Sniff Like a Dog and Experience the World in a New Way." NPR Health Shots, June 8. https://www.npr.org/sections/health-shots/2017/06/08/531744473/learn-to-sniff-like-a-dog-and-experience-the-world-in-a-new-way.

Howes, David, ed. 2005. *Empire of the Senses: The Sensual Culture Reader*. New York: Berg.

Howes, David, and Constance Classen. 2014. *Ways of Sensing: Understanding the Senses in Society*. London: Routledge

Jakubowski, Kelly, L. Stewart, S. Finkel, and D. Müllensiefen. 2017. "Dissecting an Earworm: Melodic Features and Song Popularity Predict Involuntary Musical Imagery." *Psychology of Aesthetics, Creativity, and the Arts* 11, no. 2: 122–35.

Kumai, Candice. 2018. *Kintsugi Wellness: The Japanese Art of Nourishing Mind, Body, and Spirit*. New York: Harper Wave.

Larson, Reed, and Mihaly Csikszentmihalyi. 2014. "The Experience Sampling Method." In *Flow and the Foundations of Positive Psychology: The Collected Works of Mihaly Csikszentmihalyi*, by Mihaly Csikszentmihalyi, 21–34. Dordrecht, Netherlands: Springer.

Le Breton, David. 2017. *Sensing the World: An Anthropology of the Senses*. London: Bloomsbury Academic.

Manning, Tara Jon. 2004. *Mindful Knitting: Inviting Contemplative Practice to the Craft*. Boston: Tuttle Publishing.

Nagar, Richa. 2019. *Hungry Translations: Relearning the World through Radical Vulnerability*. Urbana: University of Illinois Press.

Nakajima, Kyoko. 2015. "When My Wife Was a Shiitake." Translated by Ginny Tapley Takemori. *Words without Borders*, March 2015. https://www.wordswithoutborders.org/article/when-my-wife-was-a-shiitake.

Navarro, Tomás. 2018. *Kintsugi: Embrace Your Imperfections and Find Happiness—the Japanese Way*. London: Yellow Kite.

Oliver, Paul. 1988. "Musico-ethnological Approaches to Musical Instruments." *Popular Music* 7, no. 2: 216–18.

Oliveros, Pauline. 1974. *Sonic Meditations*. Baltimore: Smith Publications.

Pennebaker, James, and John Evans. 2014. *Expressive Writing: Words That Heal*. Enumclaw, WA: Idyll Arbor.

Pink, Sarah. 2015. *Doing Sensory Ethnography*. 2nd ed. London: Sage Publications.

Porcello, Thomas, Louise Meintjes, Ana Maria Ochoa, and David Samuels. 2010. "The Reorganization of the Sensory World." *Annual Review of Anthropology* 39:51–66.

Rechtschaffen, Daniel. 2014. *The Way of Mindful Education: Cultivating Well-Being in Teachers and Students*. New York: Norton.

Richmond-Abdou, Kelly. 2019. "Kintsugi: The Centuries-Old Art of Repairing Broken Pottery with Gold." In *My Modern Met*. https://mymodernmet.com/kintsugi-kintsukuroi/ (accessed December 29, 2019).

Santini, Céline. 2019. *Kintsugi: Finding Strength in Imperfection*. Kansas City, MO: Andrews McMeel.

Saragnano, Gennaro, and Christian Seulin, eds. 2015. *Playing and Reality Revisited: A New Look at Winnicott's Classic Work*. London: Karnac Books.

Schaeffner, André. 2016a. "About a New Systematic Classification of Musical Instruments." *Translingual Discourse in Ethnomusicology* 2 (December): 26–42.

———. 2016b. "Project for a New Classification of Musical Instruments." *Translingual Discourse in Ethnomusicology* 2 (December): 19–25.

Shelemay, Kay Kaufman. 2015. "Music and Ritual." Chap. 8 in *Soundscapes: Exploring Music in a Changing World*. 3rd ed. New York: W. W. Norton.

Silvers, Michael. 2018. *Voices of Drought: The Politics of Music and Environment in Northeastern Brazil*. Urbana: University of Illinois Press.

Smith, Linda Tuhiwai. 2012. *Decolonizing Methodologies: Research and Indigenous Peoples*. London: Zed Books.

Stoller, Paul. 1989. *The Taste of Ethnographic Things: The Senses in Anthropology*. Philadelphia: University of Philadelphia Press.

———. 1997. *Sensuous Scholarship*. Philadelphia: University of Philadelphia Press.

Thompson, Becky. 2017. *Teaching with Tenderness: Toward an Embodied Practice*. Urbana: University of Illinois Press.

Weisser, Stéphanie, and Quanten Maarten. 2011. "Rethinking Musical Instrument Classification: Towards a Modular Approach to the Hornbostel-Sachs System." *Yearbook for Traditional Music* 43:122–46.

Winnicott, D. W. 1971. *Playing and Reality*. New York: Basic Books.

Zeki, Semir. 2006. "The Neurology of Ambiguity." In *Artful Mind: Cognitive Science and the Riddle of Human Creativity*, edited by M. Turner, 243–70. Oxford: Oxford University Press.

Index

Tomie Hahn is a professor emerita of performance ethnology at Rensselaer Polytechnic Institute. She is the author of *Sensational Knowledge: Embodying Culture through Japanese Dance*.

The University of Illinois Press
is a founding member of the
Association of University Presses.

University of Illinois Press
1325 South Oak Street
Champaign, IL 61820-6903
www.press.uillinois.edu